Lockheed T-33

A Photo Chronicle

David R. McLaren

Schiffer Military/Aviation History
Atglen, PA

U.S. AIR FORCE
U.S. AIR FORCE
U.S. AIR FORCE
70708
U.S. AIR FORCE

To a T-Bird

Well, I have trod the silken heights
And traversed canyons cold and white
And spun of cloud and captive rain.
Flown through a storm, and out again.
And laughed at the dizzing ceilings gained.

Let me tell you -
We've flown grand skies so bright and clear,
You could see through time to distant years
And count the siblings of our earth
Suns and planets, in writhing birth,
Peppering the firmament - what's it worth
To see such sights, my friend?

Many nights we've flown, with moon ashine,
And left the endless miles behind.
And sought adventures in lands far, far
Away. Cleft a passage with scarce a mar,
My dancing, prancing Silver Star.

We've flung hello's to outer space.
Challenged meteorites to frantic race.
And always lost. Heard melodies slip by behind,
Wind melodies that pierced my mind.
And soothed my jet with song and sigh
Until, whispering, they bade good-bye,
And left us two to rule the sky.
My dancing Silver Star and I.

Hans Dietrich
Interceptor: October 1978

Credits

Duane "Bud" Biteman; Job Conger/Airchive; Duncan Curtis; Larry Davis; Robert Dorr; Mike Fox; David Hansen; Marty Isham; Denny Lombard; David Menard; Merle Olmsted; Doug Olson; Lionel Paul; Alain Pelletier; Dick Phillips; Jack H. Smith; Warren Thompson; Nick Williams.

Dedicated

Kaitlyn, Kyle and Eric Joseph

Book Design by Ian Robertson.

Library of Congress Catalog Number: 98-85940

Printed in China.
ISBN: 0-7643-0646-4

Published by Schiffer Publishing Ltd.
4880 Lower Valley Road
Atglen, PA 19310
Phone: (610) 593-1777
FAX: (610) 593-2002
E-mail: Schifferbk@aol.com
Please write for a free catalog.
This book may be purchased from the publisher.
Please include $3.95 postage.
Try your bookstore first.

Contents

Development

The Lockheed Aircraft Corporation TF-80C, which became the T-33, had its conception through the thoughts of Lockheed's Chief Designer, Lawrence "Kelly" Johnson. These considerations were brought on by the abysmal attrition of the early jet fighters, and not through the selfish desire to sell more aircraft. In 1946 there was an Air Force attrition rate of sixty-one aircraft per 100,000 flying hours, which was only reduced to forty in 1948 (the ten year average, 1985/1995, is 1.5!).

Prior to this time the Army Air Force/United States Air Force had only two jet aircraft with two seats. One was a Bell P-59 with an open-air cockpit installed in front of the regular cockpit that did not have even a canopy over it, while the other was a Lockheed P-80A with a rudimentary jump seat located behind the regular pilot's seat. Neither, obviously, was capable of providing anything more than an observation viewpoint for a captive observer.

During this same time frame the Air Force was experiencing the exceptionally high loss rate of aircraft, particularly due to pilot inexperience with the new jet aircraft. The accident rate was due to many factors, some being mechanical ills with the new technology of jet propulsion, while the others were brought on by the characteristics of the aircraft and the pilot's inability to deal effectively with the situation.

Strangely enough, Lockheed's Vice President in charge of military relations, V. F. Short, found it a "hard sell" to convince the Air force that a jet trainer to train new pilots, or to cross-train older ones into jet aircraft via a two-seat jet trainer, was a necessity. There was an element within the Air Force (and U.S. Navy as well) who believed that as they had been trained in conventional "tail draggers," that this was the only route to be followed by future pilots. These men had been trained through the WWII step by step concept of Primary Trainers, PT-17s, Basic Trainers, BT-13s, Advanced Trainers, AT-6s, et al, and then went into fighters or other advanced aircraft, such as P-47s or P-51s. In the immediate Post War years, those who had flown tricycled landing gear fighters during the war, such as the P-38 and P-39, were in the minority, and these aircraft had been immediately phased out of the inventory, anyhow. Yet all of the new jet aircraft were

The Lockheed YP-80A, the mother of the T-33 series, and for that matter, the father of all modern Air Force jet fighters. -Lockheed

The prototype TF-80C, 48-356, sans tip tanks. The span was 38' 10". The fuselage length 37 ft., with 14 ft. between the main landing gear and the nose wheel. It was 11' 6" to the top of the vertical stabilizer. -Lockheed

Lockheed premier test pilot Tony LeVier in a last minute consultation with a Lockheed Air Service representative before takeoff of the prototype TF-80C. LeVier passed away February 6, 1998 at age 84. This photo serves to give a good indication of the size of the TF-80C to an individual. Note the Lockheed winged star logo on the aircraft's nose. -Lockheed

equipped with tricycle landing gears. Also, at the conclusion of the war the pilot training program had done away with the Primary and Basic series of aircraft and new pilots went directly into the AT-6 Texan, although there was a new effort underway to develop a training program more akin to jet aircraft, which would result in the Beechcraft Corporation T-34 and North American Aviation T-28 with tricycle landing gears and instrument panels laid out similar to those in the jet propelled aircraft.

There were many factors that disproved the outmoded way of thinking. The tricycled landing gear of the jet fighters increased and improved visibility on the ground and was more conducive to maneuvering the aircraft, as a pilot no longer had to "S" the aircraft while taxiing, as the blind area over the aircraft's nose was no longer a factor. The runway was not obscured by the aircraft's nose while taking off, or in the landing flare and touchdown. Differential braking was enhanced.

TF-80C 48-356 with F-80C 47-173. The T-Bird's fuselage extension makes the Shooting Star appear rather stubby. -Lockheed

A major consideration was the operational characteristics of the early jet engines. They were slow to "spool-up" when the throttle was advanced, and this had to be accomplished slowly and smoothly to prevent flooding the early fuel control systems. Takeoff acceleration was quite slow in comparison to the P-47 or P-51. At the same time, landing approaches had to be anticipated with greater care, as the aircraft were harder to slow down since they did not have the drag of a propeller, while in the event of a botched approach the slow spool-up time resulted in a lack of engine response.

All of these problems notwithstanding, the Air Force still had to be convinced that a dedicated jet trainer was a necessity. To demonstrate what Kelly Johnson envisioned, Lockheed engineer Donald Palmer created a mock-up of the forward fuselage of the new trainer from a P-80's nose section in March 1947, which featured an extended canopy and two seats in tandem. Then, in May Lockheed allocated $1 million from their own funds to continue the development program. In August 1947 Johnson was able to convince the Air Force that they should "bailback" to Lockheed two P-80Cs from future production for the necessary modifications to become TP-80C.

The first of the prototype examples was P-80C 48-356 from Air Force Contract AC-16132, originally a part of an original contract of P-80C-1s allotted to the Air National Guard. Thus, the Air Force was not materially effected in their own allotments of P-80Cs. Then, under what became the new TP-80C program, the assignment fell under USAF Contract AC-19283, USAF-9, Project Air Material Command 9-PF-95. It was identified as Lockheed Model 580-74-06

Modifications to the standard P-80C airframe included a lengthening of the fuselage by 41 inches—29 inches in front of the wing's leading edge to make room for the second seat and fully equipped cockpit, and 12 inches at the wing's trailing edge to enhance lateral stability. The only concession here

A F-80C and the first of two XF-90s. The F-90 was to have been a continuation of the F-80 design, incorporating all of the proposed changes that would not fit into the smaller F-80. Its family resemblance is obvious. -Lockheed

was the reduction in size of the fuselage fuel tank from 207 gallons to 95 gallons. The new cockpit area was covered by a seven foot "clamshell" type canopy that was electrically operated and hydraulically actuated. As at this time the production P-80s were not equipped with ejection seats, neither were the initial TP-80Cs. The radio and navigational equipment would remain the same, except for an AN/A1C intercom set. The armament was reduced to two Browning M3 .50 caliber machine guns with 300 rounds per gun installed in the lower nose bay, with a K-14 gunsight mounted upon the instrument shroud in the front cockpit. As the wing was identical to that of the P-80, the "hard points" for external armament were retained. (Published reports notwithstanding, the P-80A, B, C, T-33A, F-94A and B all had this same identical wing). The required extensions to the air intake ducts and nose hydraulic systems were minor and incidental. The engine also remained the same as the P-80C (J33A-23s in the first examples), which were later replaced by J33A-25s, and later by J-33A-35s that produced 5,400 pounds static thrust.

48-356 made its first flight from Lockeed's airport at Van Nuys, California, on March 22, 1948, with Lockheed test pilot Anthony "Tony" LeVier at the controls. This TP-80C remained on bailment to Lockheed and was used to demonstrate all the aspects of it as a trainer until May 23, 1949, when it was officially accepted by the Air Force. On August 19 it then was redesignated as an ET-33A, with the "E" prefix denoting that it was "Exempt from Technical Orders." On May 22, 1950, 48-356 was modified to the prototype YF-94 and was assigned

The prototype TF-80C in flight. It became available to the Air Force on May 23, 1949, and was accepted and delivered the same day. Photographed on it's initial flight on March 22, 1948, it lacks the painted nose anti glare panel and standard buzz numbers. -Ken Mason

The second TF-80C, 48-357, actually was accepted by the Air Force long before the prototype, on August 19, 1948. On February 14, 1949 it was redesignated as an ETF-80C, (The "E" in those days denoting "Exempt from Technical Orders" and not "Electronic" as it is today.) and assigned to the 2750th Air Base Wing at Wright Patterson AFB, Ohio for ejection seat development work. The hanger in the background is presently used by the Air Force Museum for their restoration work. -Air Force Museum via Menard

48-356, the first TF-80C reincarnated as the prototype YF-94 on May 22, 1950. It continued with its original Lockheed construction number of 5001, as depicted behind the radar antenna on its nose. Its J33A engine with an afterburner fitted produced 1,400 more pounds thrust than that of the standard J33A. For more on this aircraft, consult The Lockheed F-94 Starfire, also available from Schiffer. -Farrar

to the Air Material Command's Burbank, California, Air Material Area for further development. (The second YF-94, 48-373, had been delivered to the USAF on November 24, 1948, as a TF-80C and also bailed back to Lockheed to serve in the interim as a trainer and demonstration aircraft. On March 21, 1949, it was transferred to the Culver, California, Air Material Area for the necessary radar modification by the Hughes Corporation to become the YF-94, being so designated on April 28, 1950).

The second actual TP-80C, 48-357, was made available to and accepted by the USAF on August 19, 1948, but was not actually delivered until September 16. It remained with Lockheed on bailment at Burbank, California, until February 14, 1949, when it was transferred to Wright Patterson Air Force Base, Dayton, Ohio, after being redesignated as an ETF-80C: then being assigned to the 2750th Air Base Wing, the parent unit for the Air Research and Development Command. The primary function of this example would be for the develop-

48-356 in flight as the YF-94. It remained with Lockheed until July 1954, and then was transferred to Griffiss AFB, New York for further radar development tests. Later it was placed on display at Sampson AFB, New York, and when that base was closed it was sent to Lackland AFB, Texas and hence to the Flight Test Museum at Edwards AFB, California. -McLaren collection

TF-80C-1LO (LO = Lockheed) 48-358 as assigned to the USAF's Air Material Command at Cleveland, Ohio under Project 9-PF-10 on September 7, 1948 for engine development work. It bears an overall gray paint scheme, which was unusual at this point of aircraft development. It was salvaged on February 18, 1949 after being stricken to an unknown cause. -Bowers via Olson

ment of ejection seats for both the P-80 and the future T-33As.

Finally impressed with the characteristics of the TP-80C, Lockheed was authorized by the USAF on April 7, 1948, to modify twenty-six more P-80Cs to TP-80Cs from the FY 1948 contract, 48-358/48-375 from the first portion, and 48-913/48-920 from the later. (On June 18, 1948, the Air Force redesignated their Pursuit, "P," to "F," Fighter, hence the TP-80C became the TF-80C). They also were authorized a continuation of the Fiscal Year 1949 F-80C contract for one hundred twenty-eight more examples for the USAF and sixteen more to be transferred to the U.S. Navy under the original Contract AC-19283: 49-879/1006 (49-934 was the first to be transferred to the Navy under Project NAV-OPT-9 as BuAer 124570); and 49-2757/49-2772, with 49-2758/49-2772 becoming BuAer 124571/124585. These examples, designated as TO-2s, were assigned to NAS Jacksonville, Florida, and NAS San Diego, California, to provide transition training into jet aircraft for current Navy fighter pilots. The Air Force's largess in the transferring of these aircraft to the U.S. Navy during this period is interesting and puzzling considering the political battles that were taking place at the same time: the battle for the B-36 program and the Revolt of the Admirals. With the exception of a contract for 104 further F-80Cs continuing in a final Fiscal Year 1949 contract, this marked the end of F-80 production.

Effective May 5, 1949, all existing TF-80Cs were redesignated as T-33As, and future production would reflect this

A pair of T-33A-1s of an unidentified unit showing both profile and plan forms of the aircraft in good relationship. -Lockheed

The sixth TF-80C with the F-80's "FT" Buzz Numbers and the small 175 gallon tip tanks. It has the early version of the banded canopy and no ejection seats. -Menard

An early TF-80C with its early small 175 gallon tip tanks, showing the aircraft's exceptionally clean lines. -Lockheed

change. Those destined for the U.S. Navy were now being designated as the TO-2, a continuation of the TO-1/F-80 designation. (The three F-80As, one F-80B and fifty F-80Cs transferred to the U.S. Navy were all designated as TO-1s). By the end of 1949 172 TF-80Cs/T-33As had been ordered for the USAF and USN, the last of these being delivered to the Navy on June 16, 1950.

The first T-33A assigned to the Air Training Command was 48-359 that was delivered to the 3525th Pilot Training Wing at Williams AFB, Arizona, on September 3, 1948. And then its history begins to become muddled, for it is then listed as being destroyed in an accident at McClelland AFB, California, on September 24, 1949, as well as being destroyed at Williams on November 17!

The following example, 48-360, began the T-33A's involvement with the Remote Aircraft Pilot Program. After being assigned to the 2750th Air Base Wing at Wright Patterson AFB on September 27, 1948, #360 was modified to a DTF-80C configuration on March 31, 1949, to serve as a Drone Director. After this action was completed it was transferred to Holloman AFB, New Mexico, and assigned to the 2754th Air Base Group for use in the Project Bad Boy drone program.

The Lockheed production line for the early TF-80Cs. Note that the aircraft's wingtips are rounded for the attachment of underwing tip tanks. Behind the canopy on the nearest example, observe the elevator push rods in the open plenum chamber. These were hinged on their forward ends so they could be swung up out of the way during engine maintenance. -Lockheed

A view of Lockheed's T-33 production line later on in its development. These examples now have squared-off wingtips to facilitate installation of the centerline Fletcher Aircraft Corporation tip tanks. -Lockheed

Lockheed's test pilot Anthony "Tony" LeVier with the T2V Sea Star. -Lockheed

The following 48-361 followed a similar route, but remained as a T-33.

Commencing with 48-362 that was assigned to Williams AFB on October 5, 1948, the majority of the initial T-33A production began to be assigned to the Air Training Command, and they will be covered in a separate chapter.

With a Fiscal Year 1950 contract, AC-9205, Lockheed received orders for 140 further T-33As. 50-320/50-431; 50-432, (Which had a non-sequencial construction number.) and 50-433/50-444 for 125 examples for the USAF, 50-445/50-454 for the U.S. Navy as BuAer 124930/124939, which would be the last actually delivered as TO-2s, and 50-1272/50-1276, which were delegated for transfer under the Mutual Defense Aid Pact (MDAP). However, with the advent of the Korean War in the meantime, apparently only five examples from FY 1950 were dispatched to Canada under this program. Those assigned to the U.S. Navy were also selected at random and did not adhere to the initial serial number allocations. The first deliveries of these aircraft began in July 1950 and concluded in June 1951.

Lockheed's final production area was outdoors in sunny California. Here final acceptance checks were made, specially ordered ancillary equipment added and the aircraft prepared for their initial test flight. Lockheed's production quality was to such a high standard that only one out of five T-33s, at random, actually was test flown before delivery. -Lockheed

A T-33A-5, a version without armament, close to the end of the aircraft's production run with a Fiscal Year 1958 serial number. This particular example belonged to the Air Force Systems Command, as many of the produced T-33s served in roles far removed from their training capacity. It eventually was donated to Tarrat Junior College, Ft. Worth, Texas as an instructional airframe and became registered as N93224. -Williams

The prototype T2V-1 Sea Star, Lockheed construction number 1000 with a civilian registration of N125D on its first flight December 15, 1953. -Lockheed

Fiscal Year 1951 brought three new contracts for T-33As and what the U.S. Navy now identified as the TV-2, as the U.S. Navy had revamped their aircraft identification program somewhat and Lockheed was now designated as "V" instead of "O." (Also revised under this were the PO to WV Warning Star, R6O to R6V Constitution, and R7O to R7V Constellation). These contracts, AF 14806 and AF 23071, were for FY 1951 purchases of 1,802 examples; 51-4019/51-4533; 51-6497/51-6957; 51-8506/51-9310 and 51-16976/51-16995, while AF 6578 initially was for 169 examples; and 51-17388/51-17556. However, this contract would later be extended to include 847 examples under FY 1952 funding; 52-9129/52-9975; and 94 under FY 1953 funds; 53-2687/53-2780. As previously, some were intended for the U.S. Navy and others for MDAP in specific serial number blocks, but these were not adhered to and the aircraft were pulled in a piecemeal fashion for these allocations. The initial foreign deliveries went to Belgium, Canada, France and Holland, while the later ones were to Germany, Italy and Spain.

The first production Sea Star, 142261. It bears a most attractive paint scheme. The black panels on the wing and air intake are non-skid step areas, while the black panel on the aircraft's spine houses the AN/ARN-6 radio compass antenna. -Lockheed

Cutaway view of the T2V. -Lockheed

Preparing for launch during the deck trials for the Sea Star. The NATC on the vertical fin signifies Naval Air Test Center, while the FT on the nose is for Flight Test. -Lockheed

And she's off! Identified here as the YT2V-1, although the "Y" designation does not show up on production lists. -Lockheed

1952 marked a momentary departure from the U.S. Navy's TV-2 program, as the aircraft was unsuitable for aircraft carrier operations. Lockheed thus designed their L-245 Model, later identified as the 1080-91-08 and given the U.S. Navy designation T2V-1 "Seastar." Once again this was an individual effort by the firm, and the prototype was given a civilian registration of N125. Although there was a family resemblance to the TV-2, the new version had a decidely hump-backed profile, as the rear seat had been raised six inches to enhance the instructor pilot's visibility. The new version also had leading edge wing slats and boundary layer control over the trailing edge flaps, to enhance approach and landing speeds. It also had larger empanage with increased vertical stabilizer and rudder area, as well as a relocated horizontal stabilizer with greater area. The lower aft fuselage was fitted with a tailhook for arrested carrier landings, while a catapult attachment was fitted to the forward fuselage in front of the speed brake area for deck launches. A single piece windscreen replaced the origional three-piece windshield. The original engine was the J33A-24 with 6,100 pounds st, but this was replaced on production versions with the J33A-16A at 6,350 st.

The Skyfox after the Boeing Aircraft Corporation purchased the design and changed its paint scheme from a civilian motif to that of pseudo military. It was an exceptionally clean modification of that of the T-Bird but unfortunately it stood little practical chance to make it as a viable continuation of the T-33. -Slowiak via Isham

Tony LeVier flew N125 for the first time on December 15, 1953, and found a few minor problems, mainly instability brought on by the new canopy configuration. This was rectified by enlarging the dorsal fin area. Then, in early 1954 the U.S. Navy conducted their service trials at NAS Patuxent River, and being satisfied, initially ordered eight T2Vs into production in May (BuAer 142261/142268. These were followed by 140 further examples: 142397/142399; 142533/142541; 144117/144216 and 144735/144755. A continuation of this later contract would have provided a further sixty examples, through BuAer 144824, but it as well as a contract for 180 more examples, BuAer 146058/146237, was canceled. In the interim, Lockheed also demonstrated the T2V to the USAF under a provisional designation of a T-33B, but the Air Force was satisfied with their A model and declined to accept the Seastar version. The first operational examples were delivered to the Navy on January 20, 1956, and the T2V entered "Fleet Service" on May 27, 1957, with the Naval Air Advanced Training Command at Corpus Christi, Texas.

In Fiscal Year 1953 a new contract was let, AF 22282, for a combination of T-33As, TV-2s and the newly developed RT-33A. Once again the delivery and production was at random with the 176 TV-2s and 75 RT-33As interspersed with production of the standard trainer version. They serialed 53-4886/53-5918 for 1033 T-33A-1s, and 53-5919/53-6152 for 234 T-33A-5s, which were identical to the A-1 except that they lacked the armament systems. The U.S. Navy BuAer series from this contract serialed 136793/136886, 137934/138097 and 141490/141501.

The new RT-33 had a forward fuselage fuel tank in lieu of the aft pilot's seat. Mounted on top of it was ARC-3 VHF radio equipment for utilization in areas that still did not have the

Another view of the prototype Skyfox. Note the 'bullet" on the leading edge of the horizontal stabilizer to control the airflow over both the vertical and horizontal control surfaces. -Kaston via Isham

new, standardized UHF radios, and an ARN-6 Automatic Direction Finder. In the previous forward nose armament bay were installed bays for various camera installations, normally K-14s and K-18s with various focal lengths. The new bulbous nose housed the loop antenna for the ARN-6.

The Fiscal Year 1954 contract, AF 26630, was for a combination of T-33A-1s once again, along with TV-2s and RT-33As. A total of 145 examples were produced, with 40 of these as TV-2s for the U.S. Navy, 10 as RT-33As and 95 T-33As, all for MDAP. They serialed 54-1522/1618, and of these 54-1584 and -1585 were sent to Kawasaki for assembly in Japan; 54-2689/2728 for the U.S. Navy as BuAer 138977/139016; 54-2950/54-2955 and 54-4035/54-4036.

1955 brought two separate contracts, AF 28429 and AF 30670 for a hodgepodge series of T-33A-1s, A-5s and TV-2s for a total of 268 examples with their serial numbers interspersed between the two contracts. From the first batch of 139 examples, 55-2979/55-3117, eighteen at random were sent to Kawasaki for assembly, while the series 55-2984/55-3016 and 55-3050/55-3073 went to the U.S. Navy as BuAer 141502/141534 and 141535/141558, respectively. 95 T-33A-5s serialing 55-4332/55-4426 were produced for the USAF, and 52 more as T-33A-1s for MDAP, 55-4427/55-4456; 55-4807/55-4810; 55-4945/55-4962. An addition to these contracts would have produced 79 more T-33As, 55-5155/55-5234, but these were canceled. These contracts concluded production for MDAP.

A Fiscal Year 1956 contract, AF 31212, produced 256 examples of TV-2s for the U.S. Navy and T-33A-1s and A-5s for the USAF. Of these, 220 were intended for the Air Force, 56-1573/56-1792, as T-33A-1s; and series 56-3659/56-3694 and 56-6848/56-6927 as A-5s. The 36 examples, 56-3659/56-3694 had been intended for the Navy as BuAer 143014/143049. But, as previously, the U.S. Navy TV-2s were randomly selected from the initial block of serial numbers, as they did not operate the T-33A-5 version. This contract also concluded the TV-2 production.

1957 brought Fiscal Year Contract AF 33550 for 240 T-33A-5s. A further 29 examples, 57-6308/57-6337, for T-33A-5s were canceled. All of these went to the USAF.

The last contract was for Fiscal Year 1958, AF 34659, 274 T-33A-5 examples for the USAF, 58-450/58-710 and 58-2094/58-2106. At the conclusion of production in August 1959 and the last delivery in 1960 of a T-Bird named appropriately "Exodus," a total of 5,691 T-33s had been constructed in the United States (including the twenty to Kawasaki in kit form), with 649 examples to the U.S. Navy and 1,058 delivered to foreign countries under MDAP.

Modifications to the T-33A-1 and -5 brought the -10 and -20. The T-33A-10 was essentially the same as the A-5 except that the VOR and ILS equipment was replaced by TACAN equipment.

The T-33A-20 is better known as the AT-33A, and it has the capabilities of both the T-33A-1 and -5, along with its predecessor, the F-80C. These AT-33As were pulled from existing airframes and modified to AT-33A standards as they went through IRAN (Inspect and Repair as Necessary), and there is no definitive listing of those so modified. Some of the early T-33A-1s retained their two nose .50 caliber machine guns, while those A-5s so modified carried a Lau-59 machine gun pod under each wing with a single .50 caliber in each pod. Additional armament capabilities included MA-2A rocket launchers for either 2.75 Folding Fin Aircraft Rockets, FFARs, or 5" High Velocity Aircraft Rockets, HVARs. Standard bomb

Clarence "Kelly" Johnson, the designer of the P-80, T-33, and many of the wonderful Lockheed designs that were to follow. He was the driving force behind the firm's success for decades. -Lockheed

loading was a pair of 690 pound M1116A bombs, but B37K bomb containers could be carried, as well as BDU-33 practice bombs.

Now enter the Skyfox. An attempt to revitalize the T-33 through the remanufacture of existing airframes took place in the early 1980s by the Skyfox Corporation of Los Angles, California. This involved replacing the Allison J33 engine with two Garrett TFE731-3 turbofan engines rated at 3,700 pounds of thrust and were externally mounted on the aircraft's aft fuselage. The previous two air intakes were reprofiled into the aircraft's fuselage by enlarged wing leading-edge root extensions, with winglets in lieu of the Fletcher tiptanks. To compensate for the latter, a large fuselage fuel tank was installed in place of the old engine. The empanage was also enlarged, and two new Stencel ejection seats were installed. Some seventy percent of the origional T-33 was to be retained in manufacture.

The new Skyfox spanned 37' 10", was 44' long and stood 12' 4". Its empty weight was 8,500 pounds, and takeoff gross weight was 14,400. Its initial rate of climb was 10,000 fpm, with a time to 30,000' of five minutes. Its maximum speed, however, was that of only 505 knots, or Mach .8 at altitude. With only internal fuel it had a range of 3,000 sm.

First flown on August 23, 1983, by Pat Quinn, the Skyfox earned a lot of attention, and Portugal offered a letter of intent through their Oficianas Gerais de Material Aeronautico at Alverica to build twenty examples in-country under license. However, the Boeing Aircraft Corporation purchased the rights to the design and allowed it to wither.

One last proposal to extend the service life of the T-33 was by Flight Systems Incorporated, who planned on re-engining the T-Bird with a Rolls Royce Turbomeca engine that provided an increase to 5,800 st. With the corresponding improvement in technology and a thirty percent gain in range, up to 2,400 miles was envisioned. This program also did not bear fruit.

Construction and Systems

The design of the Air Force T-33A and the U.S. Navy TV-2/T-33B derived straight-forward from 1940s era construction techniques. (For non-specific T-Bird details, a reader might consult this authors' Lockheed P-80/F-80 Shooting Star book, also available from Schiffer, as it was the progenitor for this series of aircraft.)

The nose section of the T-33 series is attached to the main fuselage by eighteen shear bolts, five flush screws, and two tension bolts. Contained in this section is the basic radio equipment, primary oxygen bottles, aircraft batteries, and, on applicable models, the armament package of two Browning M3 .50 caliber machine guns with three hundred rounds per gun. Without the four additional Brownings of the F-80 and their ammunition bins, their was enough extra room in this section to hold the ubiquitous B-4 soft-sided luggage bag. One of the stranger items to be found in this compartment is a mason jar! Originally, these jars were to catch the overflow from the lead-acid batteries that were the initial type: later, these were replaced by Nicad batteries, and the jars were retained with a solution to neutralize any spillage from them. On either side of the nose section are hinged armament bay doors, held by three sealed-bearing hinges and three latches. If these latches were not properly secured, and if these doors opened in flight, it was a major in-fight emergency. The doors would not depart the aircraft, but would open and act as a canard flying surface that disturbed the airflow over the aircraft's aft flying surfaces. If the speed boards were then opened, the aircraft would pitch down, and without available use of the elevators, the aircraft would become uncontrollable. Between the armament doors on the nose glare panel was a "yaw string" that visually indicated to the pilot the amount of slideslip/yaw experienced. The T-33 is limited to 20 degrees yaw, as the airflow across the tip tanks blank out the ailerons' authority beyond this amount.

Located below the armament bay is the nose wheel compartment. A portion of it was sealed off from the rest of the fuselage by a canvas curtain, to prevent water, slush, etc. from being thrown into the air conditioner turbine, circuit breakers, hydraulic lines, et al.

The nose wheel is of either six or eight ply, with either sixty or eighty pounds psi pressure. It is of the castering non-steerable nature, turning capability being provided by differential braking. It is said that all T-33 pilots either have, or will "cock" the nose wheel by allowing it to reach its maximum angle of forty-five degrees. This will result in the aircraft turning in circles forever, or until someone arrives to lift the

56-3659, the first of a series of Fiscal Year 1956 T-33A-5s. The white bar on the nose glare panel held a simple length of string which would slew off to the side, visually informing the pilot that the aircraft was yawing. Protruding from the aft fuselage is the bayonet or "sabre drain," which drained excess fuel from the tailpipe area. -Lockheed

51-2194 from an unidentified unit. On the leading edge of the wing, just outboard of the black painted cranked portion, is a red twelve inch triangular wedge that served to improve the aircraft's stall characteristics. -Sommerich via Lockheed

Belonging to the Air Forces' Systems Command 57-567 was later donated to the Victor Valley Community College, Victorville, California. (The home of now inactivated George AFB). Unusual are the red circles around the nose armament bay door latches. -Williams

In fine form, a Pacific Air Command Air Force T-33 departing Hickam AFB, Hawaii. The design of the entire F-80/T-33/F-94 was straight-forward and simple, which enhanced all aspects of its operation. With the exception of the later F-94C wing, the aircraft's wing for all of the above types was identical -Williams

Gear down and in the flare for landing. The distance between the main landing gear tires is 8.75 feet. The main tires are high-pressure type with channel tread, while the nose wheel is a low pressure smooth tread. (So as to not catch and then throw foreign objects into the air intakes). -Williams

aircraft's nose enough to relieve the weight off of the nose wheel and allow the nose wheel strut to be straightened.

The aft fuselage is attached to the main fuselage section with just three tension fittings, two on the upper fuselage longerons and one on the ventral longeron. Each attachment bolt is retained by a safety screw. Six further fittings retain the empennage to the aft fuselage. Contained in this area was the remote compass transmitter on the vertical stabilizer, an elevator tab actuator on the horizontal stabilizer, an aft fire warning system, and what the Navy called a "Tailpipe Joint Scupper"—referred to by the Air Force as a bayonet drain—for the removal of any residual fuel that might have pooled in the aft lower fuselage.

The wing is constructed in two sections, split down the middle for ease of repair or replacement. The airfoil is NACA 65, 213 with a chord at wing root of 110 inches and 41.89 near the wing tip. There is a 3.5 dihedral, and the early models spanned 38', 10.5" with the underslung tip tanks, while those with the Fletcher tip tanks spanned 37', 7.5". (Wing area 237.6 or 234.8, respectively). As the wing derived from a combat aircraft, the wing fuel tanks continued with semi-self sealing Fiberglas fuel tanks. Also, provisions continued for external bomb pylons (but not rocket launching stubs) via a built in bolt hole and a door for access to the inner wing to install necessary hardware and wiring.

The cockpit, or "office," is located behind a three panel windshield. The side panels are of 3/8" acrylate plastic, while the center section is 1 1/2" three-ply bulletproof glass. This was a carryover from the previous Shooting Star models, and although on the surface it does appear odd to have armored

57-609 undergoing maintenance on NASA's ramp at Los Angles, California. The plenum chamber doors have been removed for access to the J33A engine. It was later donated to the Sowela Technical Institute and registered as N82852. -Williams

Assigned to Headquarters USAF at Andrews AFB, Maryland 57-732 was utilized for proficiency flying for those pilots assigned to the Pentagon and other Washington, DC offices. The capitol dome insignia is a carry-over from the old Bolling Field insignia, which had the same supporting role before its runways were closed. The red band around the fuselage indicates the location of the engine's turbine wheel, and it was not recommended as an area to linger in when the engine was being operated, in case the J-33 started throwing turbine buckets. -Williams

AT-33A 52-9136 with eight twenty-five pound practice bombs on its pylons and a pair of practice rockets on its rocket launching racks. Inert practice ordnance is painted a medium blue for identification. -Williams

glass on a trainer, it was just as much of a necessity for pilot survival. Striking a fowl at 350 mph while in a training role easily equated to the damage that might be incurred by an enemy antiaircraft round.

The seven foot long canopy is hinged on its aft end, and over the years it went through several apparent and non-apparent modifications. Some canopies were 'banded" with a reinforcing strap at the canopy yoke in early production, while others were not, and those that were usually had these banded canopies replaced later in their service life. Beginning with the 1951 Fiscal Year contract series the canopy hinge pins were eccentric, to adjust the canopy's forward latching, and then later on in the 1951 series a second hinge point was added, along with a bungee, which further improved canopy latching at both the forward and aft ends. The canopy is normally operated electrically, but it does have both internal and external mechanical hand cranks.

The original canopy actuators were a major problem, for in the aircraft's early service life it was found that the pilots often could neither release nor jettison the canopy in an emergency situation. With the closed canopy latches electrically locked, an aircraft electrical failure left them in a locked configuration with the latches themselves binding in their receptacles. This created a situation where the canopy could neither be blown off the aircraft or opened manually via the hand crank. After a series of incidents where the pilots were trapped in their cockpits, the Air Force began equipping the cockpits with a cut down baseball bat so the pilot could beat out the Plexiglas. Later on, pilots were issued canopy knives to score the Plexiglas to cut their way out.

The initial T-33 models were built with a bare bucket-style seat, but these examples were later retrofitted with a Lockheed developed ejection seat, installed at either a modification depot, or as supplied in a kit form by Lockheed for installation

53-5404 was sent to Tinker AFB, Oklahoma to be utilized in conjunction with the Federal Aviation Administration in Project Rough Rider. This was a weather program delving into squall lines and thunderstorm research. -Isham collection

Rough Rider 53-5404 with a yaw/pitch boom on its nose and an atmospheric pressure sensor under its wing. -Not a gun pod as previously described by others. -Menard

Another view of the Rough Rider with its distinctive paint scheme. The project was a joint ARDC/NASA effort that was monitored by the FAA, which operated from Tinker AFB, Oklahoma. -Menard

at the squadron or group level. These initial ejection seats were quite limited as to versatility, and the safe "envelope" for their use was limited to the pilots having sufficient altitude and airspeeds available for their use to begin with. The pilots, initially, had to manually release themselves from the seat's shoulder and lap harness and then kick themselves clear of the seat itself before opening their parachute. As further ejection seat development occurred, improved seats were built and retroactively installed in line aircraft. These new seats included automatic seat harness releases with automatic parachute activation and improved canopy ejection/seat firing capabilities for effective use at lower airspeeds and altitudes. The final seat was of the rocket-ejection method, with a zero delay lanyard attached that permitted ejection at any altitude as long as 125 knots airspeed had been attained (Or at 125 knots at a minimum altitude of 125 feet, if the lanyard was not attached).

One major consideration of the front seat pilot's seating in the T-Bird is that of an emergency egress. Due to the relationship of the front ejection seat to the instrument panel and the windscreen bow, pilots of certain heights and wearing certain survival equipment cannot safely eject from the front

AT-33A-20LO 53-5270 with nose installed .50 caliber machine guns and underwing pylons. Although designed to be able to carry machine guns on the pylons, there was no hard and fast rule that this was all-exclusive. Oddly enough, as the F-80 was being disposed of at the same time as the AT-33 was devised, there appears to be no attempt to attach a F-80s nose to the T-33 airframe to increase its armament. This might have been due to an adverse affect upon the aircraft's center of gravity? -Williams

52-9375 had a F-94C nose attached. This T-Bird was supplied to the Hughes Aircraft Corporation on bailment, for development of the Starfire's weapons system. -Bishop via Isham

Another nose modification was to 51-4120, which with the F-94A nose grafted, became an NT-33A. This example became the longest serving T-33 in the United States military, even though it spent most of its service life on bailment to Cornell University. -Isham

cockpit without sustaining major injury to themselves. A pilot that is 5' 7" tall will clear the windshield bow by four inches, unless he is wearing a back pack dinghy and has a tendency to slouch in the seat, for upon ejecting his knees will strike the windshield bow. Likewise, a tall torsoed pilot wearing a seat type parachute will be safely ensconced, where a long-legged pilot wearing a backpack parachute is in harms way. Before the T-Bird was phased out of USAF/ANG service the potential front seat pilots were screened for cockpit clearance, and if they didn't fit, they were relegated to the back seat.

The aircraft instrumentation and ancillary cockpit equipment varied with the various aircraft Block Series. It was said that when a new instrument was to be installed in the T-33, the mechanic placed it where ever it would fit, and no two instrument panels were ever exactly alike. This did not help the pilot's instrument scan! One of the odd remnants of the early jet era remaining in the T-33 cockpit is that the fuel totalizer counter is calibrated to gallons of fuel remaining, instead of pounds as found on later jet aircraft. As antiquated as it is, however, it does make it easy for the pilot to ascertain his range, as the general rule-of-thumb equated one mile of range per gallon (at normal cruising altitudes). Equally antiquated in appearance is the landing gear handle, as it is simply a curved rod with a ball on the end of it—its shape did make confirmation of its identity apparent on those "dark and stormy nights" when the pilot was making an instrument approach and didn't dare take his eyes off his flight instruments, though. In application, when the landing gear handle was moved to the down position, it was given a "jiggle check," just to make sure that it had enough free travel to successfully lower the wheels.

Navigation and radio equipment went through many changes as technology and demands changed over the years. The initial radio transmit/receive equipment was the SCR-522 four-channel (plus the 121.5 emergency frequency) VHF

Another view of 51-4120 as the NT-33A. It was retired in April 1997 and now belongs to the Air Force Museum, Dayton, Ohio. -Curry via Conger

56-3674 assigned to Edwards AFB, California. The Fletcher tip tanks held 230 gallons, JP-4 being the standard fuel. -Williams

NT-33A 49-913 of the Air Research and Development Command, Wright Air Development Center, Dayton, Ohio. Note that the nose contour has been modified, as well as the armament bay door. It appears to have a camera faring behind the nose wheel doors. -Norm Taylor

The nose gear landing strut of a T-33A with torque link and landing lights. -Conger

radio, which was hampered by both a limited range and atmospheric conditions. These were replaced by the AN/ARC-27 eighteen channel (plus the 243.0 emergency frequency) UHF radio that had far superior reception range that was less hampered by atmospheric conditions. Initially, both of these radios were installed on the pilot's right console, but during the last major change the "control heads" were placed upon the main instrument panel, which permitted the pilot to change, or retune, radio frequencies without having to turn his head. This reduced the propensity to encounter vertigo, or the "leans."

Located on the lower portion of the instrument panel in front of the control stick on the early models was the AN/ARA-6 radio compass control head for the operation of Low/Medium frequency navigational equipment, as for the use of the LF/MF four-course radio ranges and Homers. As progression took place, these were replaced by Visual/Aural (VOR) equipment, and then by AN/ARN-21 TACAN (Tactical Air Navigation) equipment that provided for range/bearing and distance information.

The T-33, like the F-80, was the "stealth" of its day, since due to its small cross section it provided an extremely limited radar return. Until the creation of the MTI (moving target indicator), it was almost impossible to pick one up on the early radar equipment, and in areas of precipitation, temperature inversion, or "grass" ground clutter, it indeed was an impossible event. As An/APX-6 IFF (Identification, Friend or Foe) sets became available in the early 1950s they were added to the T-33/TV-2, but not until tactical requirements had been met, which meant that a lot of lost aircraft were never found on radar in emergency situations. Eventually, again, the old IFF was replaced by AN/APX-72 transponders, which pro-

The landing gear doors of the T-33 with a portion of the main doors missing. The panel hanging down is open to permit access to the bottom of the engine. -Hansen

A T-33As main landing gear, showing the landing gear door retraction link. -Conger

Main landing gear doors of a T-33A. -Conger

An air intake of a T-33 showing boundary layer splitter and vent. -Conger

Tail pipe exhaust of a T-33A with aft navigation lights, amber on the top, white on the bottom, which alternated in flashing sequence (When not on steady, as dictated by the pilot). -Conger

Allison J33A engine of a T-33A. -Conger

A 183rd TFG T-33A dismantled for periodic inspection. -Conger

Forward windscreen of a T-33A. -Conger

The seven foot long canopy of a T-33A. Embedded in the aft portion is the Command Radio antenna. -Conger

The aft portion of a Fletcher T-33A tip tank. The fin stabilized the tank under aerodynamic loads, which prevented wing twisting and resultant wing failure, which occurred on other types of aircraft before such fins were installed on their tanks. -Conger

The forward portion of a Fletcher tip tank showing the fuel filler cap. The jettison preventing retaining pin is installed. -Conger

Not a pleasant sight, but interesting for the view of the nose bulkheads. The remains of 51-8714 at Hickam AFB. -Williams

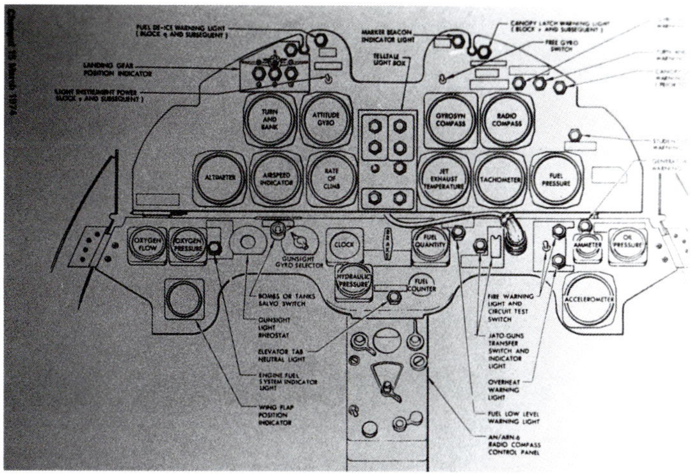

T-33 Front instrument panel

vided both radar mode and code, along with altitude encoding.

The forward cockpit is fitted with an aileron boost switch that permits the pilot to adjust the hydraulic boost to the ailerons in degrees between one and eight, with optimum at six. With the boost full on, the T-Bird is far too responsive, and many fledgling pilots commented on never being able to stay up with the aircraft's rate of roll.

The T2V/T-1A Sea Star

The Sea Star was a logical follow-on to the T-Bird and incorporated many improvements brought on by another decade of learning and technology. Although maintaining a family resemblance to the earlier series, the Sea Star was an entirely new aircraft in most respects.

The length of the T2V/T-1A was 36' 7", a reduction of one foot, one inch from the T-33A/TV-2. The new wing spanned 42' 11", an increase of five feet. Its height was increased by one foot, four inches. The empty weight had increased by three thousand pounds, while likewise, the takeoff weight was also increased by five thousand pounds, from 11,965 to 16,600.

Although the T2V/T-1A continued with the J33 series engine, the improved J33A-24 in the Sea Star provided 6,100 pounds thrust, an increase of seven hundred pounds thrust over that of the J33A-25 (or -35) installed in the T-33A/TV-2. This increased the aircraft's maximum speed to 580 mph, versus 543 mph in the T-Bird. However, the increased aircraft's weight did reduce its service ceiling down from 47,500 feet to 40,000 feet.

As the Sea Star was designed for aircraft carrier capabilities, it featured a hydraulically retractable tailhook, as well as a hold-back catapult hook located just forward of the arrestor hook and a catapult attachment point just in front of the dorsal speed brakes. It also had a supplementary set of speed brakes located, one on each side, aft of the wings'

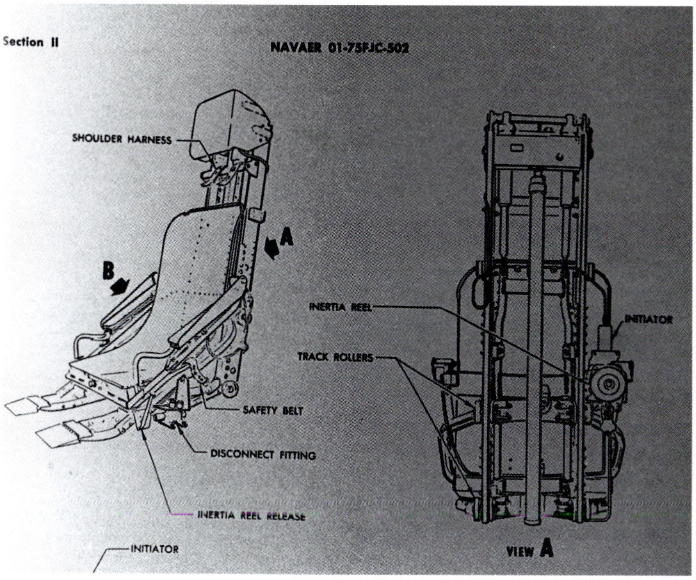

Mid series T-33A ejection seat.

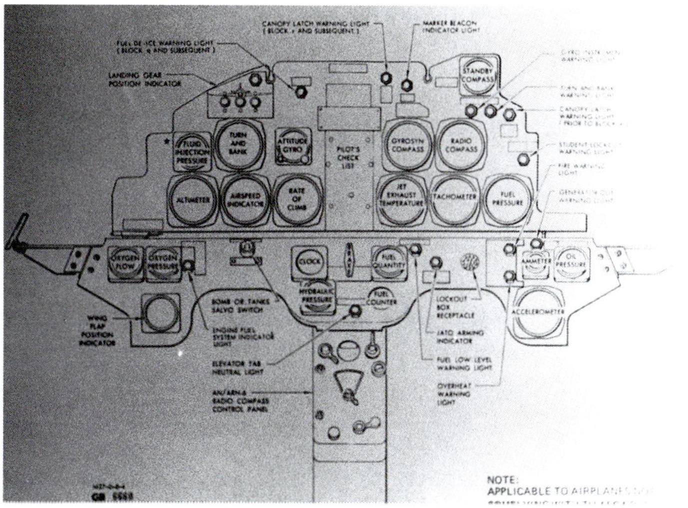

T-33 aft instrument panel

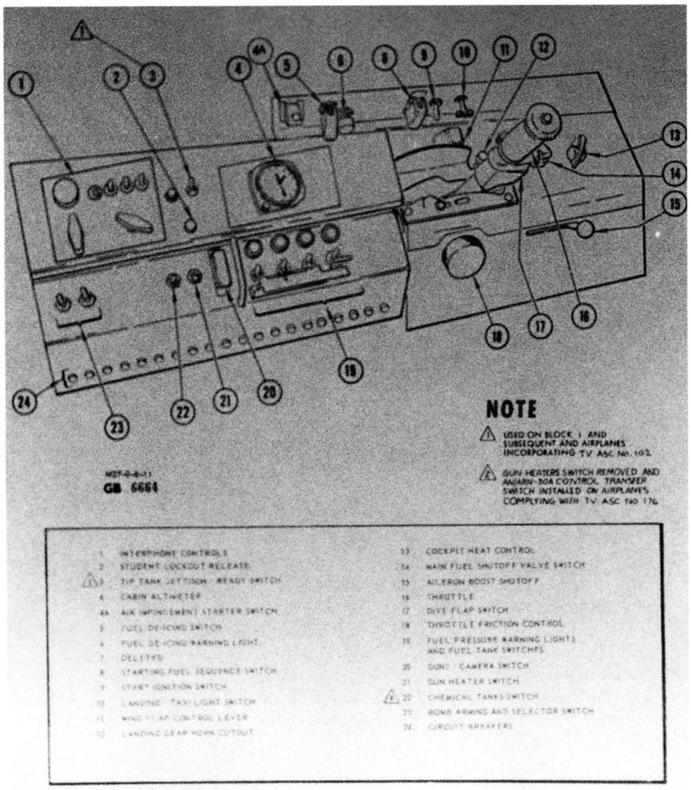

T-33 left pilots console

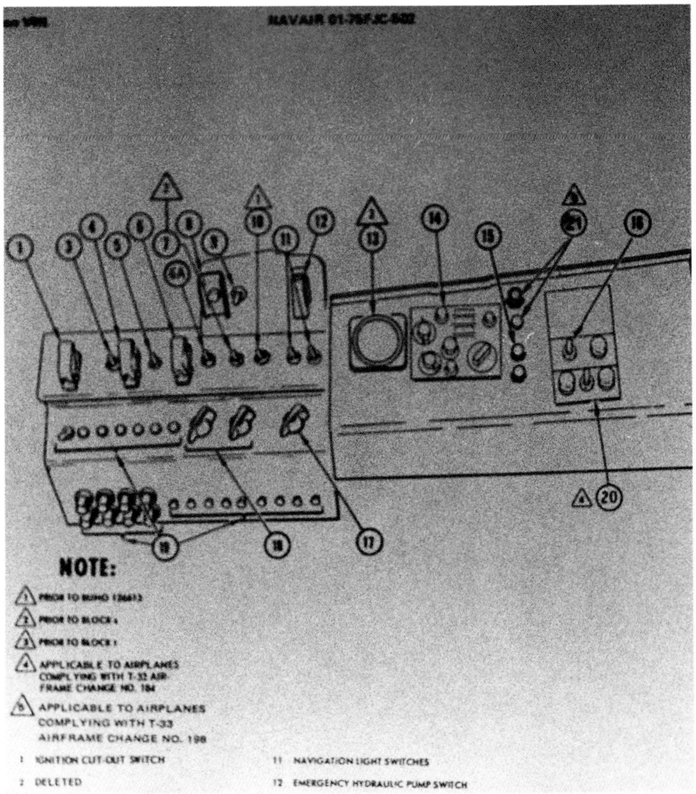

T-33 right pilots console

T2V forward pilots instrument panel

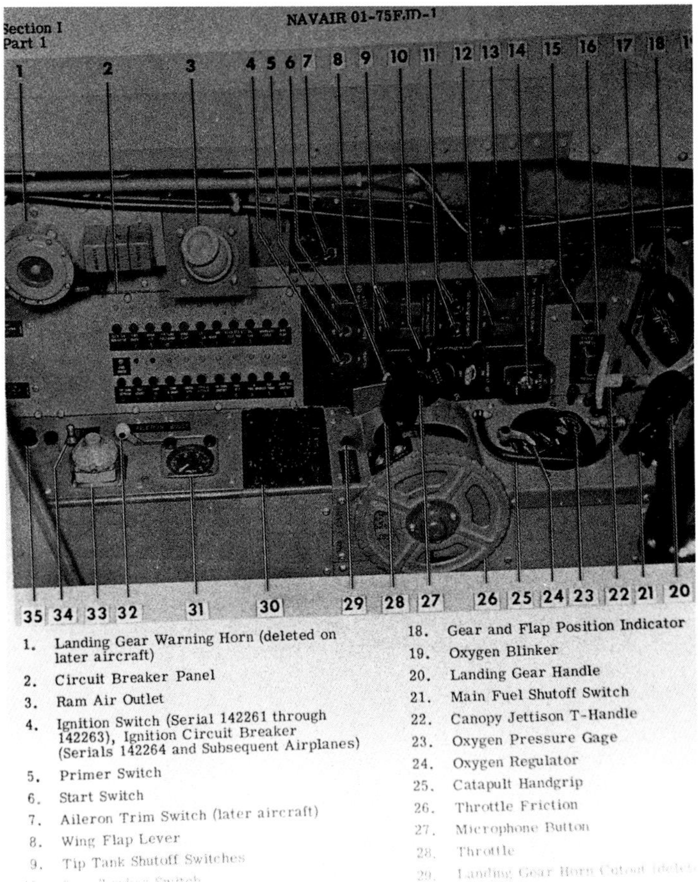

T2V forward pilots left console

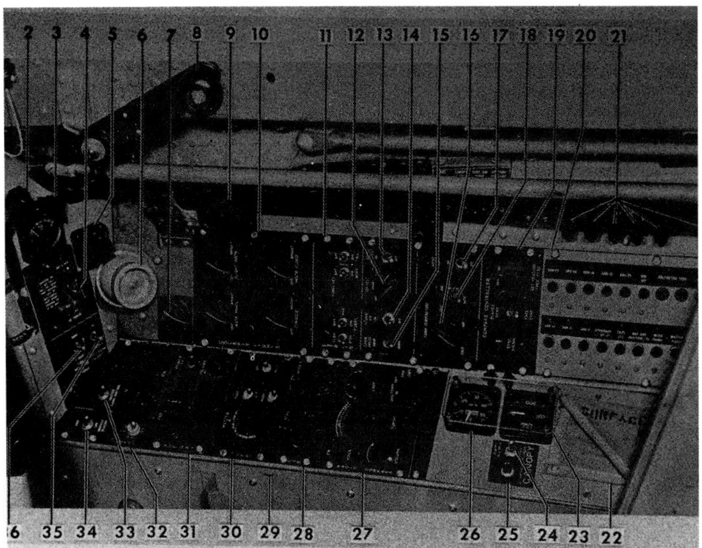

1. Map Light
2. Arresting Hook Handle
3. Voltmeter
4. Battery-Generator Switch
5. Loadmeter
6. Pressure Air Inlet
7. Approach Indexer Rheostat
8. Canopy Lock Handle
9. Floodlight
10. Cockpit Lighting Panel
11. Exterior Lights Panel
12. Normal Defrost Control
13. Auxiliary Defrost Control
14. Cabin Air Switch
15. Cabin Pressure Dump Switch
16. Cabin Temperature Selector
17. Pitot Heat Switch (Circuit Breaker)
18. Cabin Temperature Override Switch
19. S-2 Compass Controller
20. Circuit Breaker Panel
21. Fuses
22. Surface Control Lock Stowage
23. Hydraulic Pressure Gage
24. Canopy Close Switch
25. Canopy Open Switch
26. Cabin Pressure Altimeter
27. AN/ARN-6 Control Panel
28. AN/APA-89 Coder
29. Map Case
30. AN/APX-6B Identification Control
31. AN/ARN-14E VHF Receiver
32. AN/ARN-21 DME Control Panel
33. Master Radio Control Switch and Indicator Light
34. AN/ARN-12 Marker Beacon Sensitivity Switch
35. Anticollision Lights Switch
36. A.C. Flight Instrument

T2V forward pilots right console

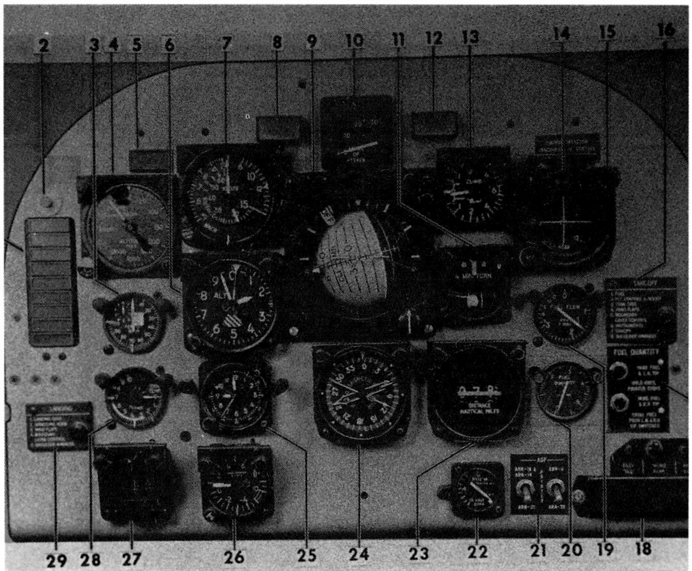

1. Annunciator Warning Panel
2. Annunciator Panel Test Switch
3. Tachometer (% R.P.M.)
4. AN/APN-22 Radio Altimeter Indicator
5. Landing Gear Warning Light*
6. Altimeter
7. Airspeed Indicator (Machmeter)
8. Aft Overheat Warning Light
9. B1-A Attitude Indicator
10. Angle of Attack Indicator
11. Turn and Slip Indicator
12. Plenum Fire Warning Light
13. Vertical Velocity Indicator
14. ID/249 Cross-Pointer Indicator
15. AN/ARN-12 Indicator Light
16. Takeoff Checklist
17. Fuel Quantity Indicator Switches
18. Tell-Tale Light Indicator
19. Fuel Flowmeter
20. Fuel Quantity Indicator
21. ID/250 Pointer Selector Switches
22. Elevator Trim Indicator
23. ID/310 Distance Indicator
24. ID/250 Radio Magnetic Indicator (
25. Eight-Day Clock
26. Accelerometer
27. Standby Compass
28. Exhaust Temperature Indicator
29. Landing Checklist

*BuAer Serials 144125 and up; also earlier aircraft that have incorporated BuAer T2V ASC No. 7

T2V aft pilots instrument panel

trailing edge. To prevent damage to the aircraft in the event of an arrestor barrier engagement, a pitot mast was located just in front of the nose landing gear.

Since the aircraft was intended for aircraft carrier operations from the onset, there was no continuity from the previous models, and the entire instrument panel and most of the cockpit layout was different. Featured were an angle of attack instrument (AOA), and this was coupled with an Approach Indexer, which provided electronic indications for pilot reference to his proper approach attitude angles without demanding distracting navigational instrument scans from the usual instrument panel. The T2V/T-1A did utilize the usual communications and navigational equipment of the previous series.

For emergency egress, the canopy was provided with the usual explosive charge for its removal. A major change, though, incorporated the use of the Martin-Baker Mark L-5 ejection seats. These twelve part seats were usable at any altitude as long as a minimum of 100 knots airspeed was available. The seats carried their own two drogue parachutes, a 22" controller and a five foot stabilizing chute, as well as an automatic g force limiter that prevented the pilot's own para-

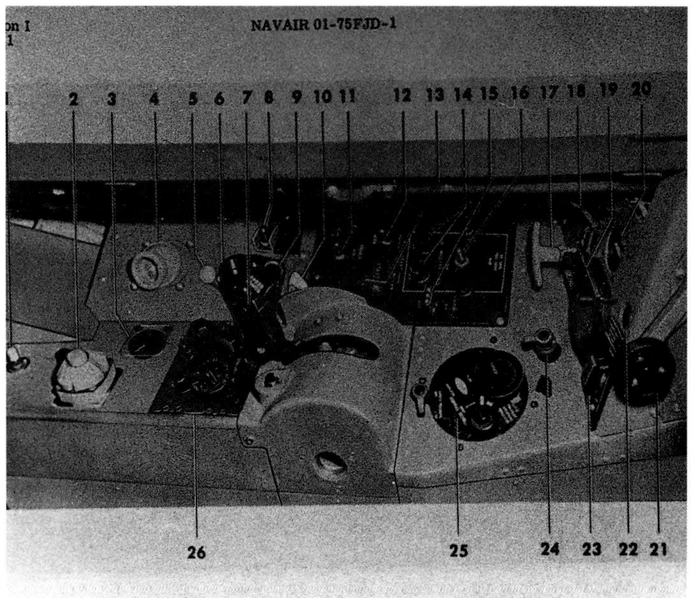

Canopy Jettison Cylinder Charging Valve
G-Suit Control Valve
15. Landing Light Switch
16. Tip Tank Fuel Dump Switch
17. Canopy Jettison T-Handle

T2V aft pilots left console

1. Battery-Generator Switch
2. Loadmeter
3. Canopy Latch Indicator
4. Master Radio Control Panel
5. AN/ARN-14E VHF Receiver
6. AN/ARN-21 DME Control Panel
7. Pressure Air Inlet
8. AN/ARN-6 Control Panel
9. Cockpit Lighting Panel
10. Circuit Breaker Panel
11. Canopy Close Switch
12. Canopy Open Switch

T2V aft pilots right console

chute from opening until after an acceptable g force had been reached. Likewise, the pilot was restrained by the seat during high altitude bailouts until the barostatic control released him at an acceptable altitude, "So that the occupant can quickly descend through the rarefied atmosphere before the parachute opens." The main activation method was through the Navy's preferred "face curtain" method, although their was a secondary firing handle between the pilot's legs.

The new fuel system was of the single-point type, requiring but one refueling receptacle for ground servicing. The tip tanks were of the non-jettisionable type, having built in fuel dumping capabilities in case of an emergency. It was found that the entire series flew much better with the tip tanks installed than without them. The tanks themselves provided sufficient lift to overcome the drag of their frontal area, and they provided a boundary airflow over the outer wings and ailerons which enhanced both lift and aileron authority.

Specifications

	T-33A/T-33B (TV-2)	T2V (T-1A)	T-33A(N) Canadair
span	39' 11"	42' 11"	39' 11"
length	37' 9"	36' 7"	37' 9"
height	11' 4"	12' 11"	11' 4"
empty weight	8, 084	11, 400	8, 200
takeoff weight	11, 965	16, 600	16, 800
Maximum speed	524 mph	580 knots	570 mph
service ceiling	47, 500	40, 000	47, 000
optimum range	1300 s.m.	970 s.m.	1, 040 s. m.

The view from the rear seat of the T-Bird was limited by all sorts of obstructions, mainly that of the front pilot's ejection seat, of which this particular model has the latest seat fitted with the built-in canopy breaker. -S/Sgt. David McLeod via Dorr

USAF/Naval Air Training

At the conclusion of WWII it was decided by Air Force planners that the old concept of Primary, Basic and Advanced pilot training was obsolete, as a fledgling pilot could learn to fly just as readily in an aircraft at 155 mph as in one at 95 mph. Thus, the open cockpits of the PT-17 and the rattling canopies of the BT-13 were done away with, and pilot training now commenced with the North American Aviation AT-6, which was correspondingly redesignated as simply the T-6.

After an initial orientation to the military way of life and final mental and physical evaluations, the to be student pilot was assigned to an Air Training Command base, these bases being located primarily in either the southeast or southwestern portions of the United States, for their usually more fair weather conditions. These included the following: Connally, Goodfellow, or Perrin Air Force Bases, Texas; civilian contract schools at Columbus or Greenville, Mississippi—After the Korean War started additional civilian contract pilot schools were added, one being located as far north as Malden, Missouri—Circa 1952 these were at Bainbridge and Moultrie, Georgia; Bartow, Florida; Hondo, Texas; Marana, Arizona; Kinston, North Carolina; and Greenville and Columbus, Mississippi. The only active participating USAF base at this time was Goodfellow AFB, Texas, as Perrin had been turned over to the Air Defense Command.

50-387, as assigned to "How" flight (Under the old phonetic alphabet.) of the 3525th Pilot Training Wing at Williams AFB, Arizona under Project TRC-1PT-222 on January 2, 1951. On June 4,1952 it was transferred to the 3530th PTW at Bryan AFB, Texas, and it was written off in an accident on August 17, 1952. -Bowers via Olson

48-370 was assigned to "The Fighter School," the 3525th PTW at Williams AFB on December 1, 1948. In 1954 it was assigned to Lackland AFB's 3700th MITW. A little known unit at an air base little known for flying operations. -USAF via Menard

A pair of 3560th Pilot Training Wing T-Birds flying out of Webb AFB, Texas. -via Menard

After some twenty hours of dual instruction in the T-6 the student pilot was expected to solo or be terminated. Then, after an additional 130 hours of a combination of dual and solo flight, which included formation, aerobatics, basic instruments and night flying, students moved up to the T-28A intermediate trainer that was just entering the inventory for more advanced training. (Pilots selected for multi-engine aircraft progressed from the T-28A to the TB-25). After some 265 hours of flight over a period of twelve months the student pilot was commissioned as a 2nd Lieutenant and received his wings. This was followed by proceeding on to either the F-51D or H, or to the new jet fighters, the F-80, F-84 or F-86, and upon graduation the new pilot was assigned to an active Air Force command. (The F-51 was withdrawn from the Air Training Command in 1953, the T-6 in July 1956).

A Nellis based T-33A with standardized Air Training Command markings. -Menard

50-404 was delivered to Nellis AFB, Nevada on March 4, 1951 and assigned to the 3595th Pilot Training Wing's 3598th Pilot Training Squadron. -via Minert/Isham

50-417 from the first batch of T-33A-1LOs. It had previously served with the 3525th PTW, and then assigned to the 3520th Combat Crew Training Wing at Wichita, Kansas. Later it went to the 3625th PTW at Tyndall AFB, Florida. The underslung tip tanks contain 165 gallons of fuel, and are based upon the Misawa tanks developed in Japan just prior to the Korean War. -Paul

51-4489 of the 3525th PTW with the early non-banded canopy. It became a display aircraft at Murray, Utah. -Paul

U.S. Navy student pilots followed a similar program as that of the USAF, while the initial Marine Corps syllabus differed by sending the student pilot through the basic Marine Corps Ground Officer training program first, as the USMC believes that their pilots' first responsibility is to those Marines on the ground, and their pilots were never to forget their origin.

Navy and Marine student pilots initially started with the SNJ, the naval version of the T-6, in Basic Training Unit 1 at Naval Air Station Whiting Field, Florida. They then proceeded to BTU-2 at Corry Field for night and initial instrument training, and then to BTU-3 at Saufley Field to learn formation and gunnery techniques. With this behind them, they were assigned to BTU-4 at NAS Pensacola to commence learning aircraft carrier landing techniques, both simulated at Pensacola and actual landings aboard an aircraft carrier offshore. As time progressed the Navy intoduced the T-28B to replace the SNJ. The T-28B was a superior version of the T-28A with a larger engine and (for that time) high altitude capabilities, including an aerodynamic speed brake. Moving on to NAS Corpus Christi, Texas, the student pilot was introduced to the TV-2, in which he flew 120 hours before moving on to tactical aircraft types, such as the TV-1 Shooting Star or the F9F Panther, before returning to Pensacola for final aircraft carrier qualifications before joining a Fleet squadron.

With the assignment of the T-33A to the Air Training Command under Project TRC-3T-20, USAF-20, T-33s were initially assigned to the 3525th Pilot Training Wing at Williams

50-439 was assigned to the 3520th CCTW at Wichita, Kansas on June 20, 1951 after previous service with the 3525th PTW. The primary mission of the 3520th CCTW was to provide jet transition training for B-29 pilots preparing to fly the B-47. It was reassigned to the 3550th CCTW at Moody AFB, Georgia on March 16, 1954. -Sommerich via Olson

51-6804 belonged to the 3645th Combat Crew Training Wing at Laughlin AFB, Texas. The "A" suffix to the buzz number was added if there was more than one of the given type with the same last three digits to its serial number, but these were unusual to see on any aircraft other than the F-84. -McLaren collection

T-33As of the 3520th PTW out of Wichita. Most Air Training Command T-Birds were pretty well nondescript in paint schemes. -Isham

51-8784 belonged to Tyndall AFB's 3626th Combat Crew Training Wing. Note that the angle of the lowered flaps closely paralleled that of the deployed speed brakes. -Martin via Pickett/Isham

52-9237 belonged to the 3550th CCTW at Moody AFB, Georgia. This unit was closely connected to Air Defense Command requirements and concentrated on instrument flying techniques. -Isham

50-375 belonged to the 3550th Fighter Training Wing at Moody AFB. The vertical fin is red with white lightening flashes. -Menard

T-33As of the 3535th PTW out of Vance AFB, Oklahoma during a steep turn. -Isham

Air Force Base, Arizona, in 1948. Then, as more T-33s became available they were assigned to the following Wings and Air Force Bases in numerical order: 3605th PTW at Greenville AFB, Mississippi; 3510th PTW at Randolph AFB, Texas; 3530th PTW at Bryan AFB, Texas; 3540th PTW at Pinecastle (later McCoy) AFB, Florida; 3560th PTW at Webb AFB, Texas; 3565th PTW at James Connally AFB, Oklahoma; 3580th PTW at Foster AFB, Texas; 3615th PTW at Craig AFB, Alabama; 3640th PTW at Laredo AFB, Texas; and the 3645th PTW at Laughlin AFB, Texas.

As the USAF expanded with the demands of both the Korean War and the Cold War, additional ATC T-33 bases were added under the creation of the new Flying Training Air Force (FTAF), which was established on May 1, 1951. The 3500th PTW at Reese AFB, Texas; 3520th PTW at Wichita (later McConnell) AFB, Kansas, until June 1952 when the 3520th switched to B-47s and became concerned with training new B-47 crews; 3535th at Mather AFB, California; 3575th at Vance AFB, Oklahoma; and the 3635th at Stead AFB, Utah.

Once the initial training had been accomplished, USAF pilots moved on to T-33 bases dedicated to the pilots gaining command. Those going to the Strategic Air Command were assigned to the 3500th PTW at Barksdale AFB, Louisiana, or the 4240th Fighter Training Wing at Pinecastle/McCoy AFB. Those destined for the Air Defense Command were assigned to the 3625th PTW at Tyndall AFB, Florida; the 3550th at Moody AFB, Georgia, or the 3555th PTW at Perrin AFB, Texas. The 3595th PTW at Nellis AFB, Nevada, and the 3600th at

52-9254 belonged to an unknown ATC unit. The gray vertical fin tip contained the AN/ARC-3 VHF or AN/ARC-27 UHF radio antenna. Just above the tail pipe orifice is the amber and white navigation lights which usually alternated in sequence. -Lockheed

Another view of 52-9254 with -9252. Three fourths to the rear of the Fletcher tip tanks are tear-drop shaped navigation lights, red on the left, green on the right. These are controllable by the pilot as to brightness and in steady or flashing mode. -Lockheed

Photo of T-33A-I-LO 53-4937 at Dayton Airport, September 1954. -Warren Shipp.

58-578 of TAC's 4430th CCTS, but still bearing the insignia of the 354th Tactical Fighter Wing on its fuselage. -Isham

An Acrojet T-33A from the 3525th PTW. It eventually went to the 2469th Flying Training Wing at Scott AFB, Illinois for use by the Air Force Reserve. -Menard

The USAF Acrojets from Williams AFB, Arizona circa 1952. When the USAF decreed in 1953 that the team needed to fly their routines with tip tanks installed, they decided to disband, as they believed that the tanks derogated their performance. -Lockheed

The Acrojets snugged in tight. Whereas they previously had dedicated F-80s with markings identifying their aircraft as belonging to the acrobatic team, after they converted to T-33s their aircraft were in the nondescript Air Training Command scheme. -Lockheed

T-33As of the 95th Fighter Interceptor Training Squadron, Tyndall AFB, Florida, the last major Air Defense Command user of the T-Bird. -Isham

51-4076 was the support-ship for the famed Thunderbirds and used for general hack work as well as giving politicians and the media a ride in a jet. Later the "Thunderbirds" on the fuselage was changed from block style to script. -Esposito

The Lackland AFB, Texas Military Training Center "Warhawks." They were led by Lt. Colonel Demetrios Karnezius. Lead pilot was Captain Richard Able; Left Wing was 1st Lt. William Phillips; Right Wing was Captain William Underwood; Slot Pilot was Captain Fred Haeffner; and Alternate was Captain Robert Baird. -via Menard

The Warhawks during a formation takeoff. When the runway at Lackland AFB was closed, the Warhawks moved their operations to Kelly AFB, which joined Lackland. -via Menard

A Warhawk formation landing at Kelly AFB. After the move from Lackland the Warhawks obtained their T-Birds from the Air Force Logistics Center at Kelly, instead of the Air Training Command. -via Menard

Luke AFB, Arizona, were dedicated to the Tactical Air Command. Likewise, with the expansion of the FTAF, some units were transferred in their roles, as the 3605th PTW moved to Ellington AFB, Texas, from Greenville, Mississippi, and became an Observer Training Wing in 1952.

The undergraduate training program had been forecasted to provide 3,000 pilots a year in 1951, but oddly enough there were not enough qualified applicants and only 2,300 pilots were graduated. Then, in 1951 the USAF obtained Congressional approval for ninety-five Wings, and hoped for 7,200 pilots per year commencing in January 1952. Even though there was an influx of student pilots, brought on by enthusiasm for flying as a result of the Korean War, these goals fell well short, with only 2,702 graduates in Fiscal Year 1952 and 4,595 in FY 1953. In part, the pipeline was delayed by a lack of suitable trainers! Then came the authorized expansion to 143 Wings, but the best that the Crew Training Air Force was able to produce was 5,315 pilots in FY 1954, which was followed by a meager 2,633 in FY 1955, and a high of 5,701 in FY 1956.

In Lockheed's favor, and the Air Force's increased emphasis on flying safety, by this same time the aircraft accident rate had fallen to fifteen major accidents per 100,000 flying hours in 1956. For those who did not believe that jets were safer than props, the 1921 rate was 467 accidents per 100, 000 hours.

Budget reductions for Fiscal Year 1958 reduced the Air Training Command's portion by $75 million dollars. The USAF dropped its pilot training requirements to just 2,700 individuals. Part of this was brought on by the USAF being able to retain personnel, and the other portion by actual lowered pilot demands. In 1958 ATC transferred Nellis, Luke and Williams AFBs to the Tactical Air Command; McConnell went to the Strategic Air Command, and Ellingtion AFB to the Continental Air Command. This action left but five flying training wings and five pilot training wings. Several ATC bases, such

TV-2t 137936 (USAF 53-5243), construction number 8224, was the last of this particular Block Series. Notable is that its flaps are partially lowered and that the rarely seen plenum chamber doors are open to suck more air into its engine. The back seater seems to be enjoying his ride. It became a display aircraft at Pueblo, Colorado -Lockheed

141490 (USAF 53-5706) was a TV-2ab that belonged to VU-7 from Naval Air Station San Diego, California. "VU" translates as "heavier than air-utility," a catch-all term. The purpose of the tear drop shape under the aft fuselage is unknown, but may be an IFF antenna? -USN via Dorr

TV-2 143017 (USAF 56-1659) now identified as a T-33B , hence photographed after 1962, in its landing flare with an apparent unusually high angle of attack. -McLaren collection

TV-2y 141528 (USAF 55-3010) photographed at NAS Willow Grove, Pennsylvania in 1956. The lack of a prefix number indicates that the aircraft belonged to a regular navy unit, instead of reserve. -Esposito

as Bryan and the 3530th PTW, were inactivated, and the the civilian pilot training program commenced to be phased out.

In 1959 the USAF shifted its emphasis from a specialized to generalized pilot training, where each pilot was considered to be universally assignable between single or multi-engined aircraft. The pilot "production goal" was reduced to just 1,500 pilots. In 1960 Williams AFB returned to the ATC after the transfer back from the Tactical Air Command, once again recreating the 3525th Pilot Training Wing.

Not all T-33Bs remained stateside. 138065 (USAF 53-5666) photographed at Atsugi, Japan with standard 1960 era markings. -unknown

T-33B 141525 (USAF 55-3007) with a gloss-gray paint scheme for corrosion prevention. The "7B" denotes the Naval Air Reserve Squadron at NAS Atlanta, Georgia. -Paul

A TV-2, 141541 (USAF 55-3056) photographed at NAS Olathe, Kansas. Olathe was one of the first Naval Air Stations closed by edict of R. Strange McNamara and it became a municipal airport and housing area for the not so well off. -Gosney via Esposito

By 1962 the T-33 was destined for replacement by the Northrop T-38 Talon after fourteen years of service with the Air Training Command. In the intervening years the USAF had replaced the T-28 Trojan with first the Beechcraft T-34 Mentor, and then the Cessna T-37 "Tweet" was slated to replace the T-34 entirely. By this time the program had provided for 130 hours in the T-34, T-37 and T-33 before progressing to either the F-86F or F-100, but it was envisioned that by combining the three types into the T-37 and increas-

TV-2 137981 (USAF 53-5451) as assigned to ATU-205 at NAS Pensacola, Florida. Photographed at NAS Moffett Field, California May 17, 1958. -Larkins via Olson

TV-2 136828 (USAF 53-3722) belonged to Marine Air Squadron 24. Note that the machine gun port is open, although no armament or gunsight is installed. -Balogh via Olson

Another TV-2, this time from NAS Kingsville, Texas. 138006 (USAF 53-5523) belonged to Advance Training Squadron 7. -Balogh via Olson

131777 (USAF 51-8741) belonged to Marine Air Squadron 32. The fuselage placement of the National Insignia is unusual. -Rankin via Olson

The support TV-2 for the US Navy Blue Angles was BuAer 128-662 (USAF) 51-4240). Note the open gun ports. The scheme has since shown up on several civilian T-Birds. -Shipp via Olson

ing the number of flying hours to 140 a total saving of $15,598.00 per student would be gained. (The cost per flying hour per student being given as $190.00). The T-33As were phased out from the following bases in the following order: 3560th at Webb; 3500th at Reese; 3575th at Vance; 3640th at Laredo; 3550th at Moody; 3525th at Williams; 3646th at Laughlin; and 3510th at Randolph. The 3615th PTW at Craig was the last USAF Air Training Command unit, not completely phasing out the T-33A in this role until 1967.

Also in October 1962 the United States military undertook a redesignation system of their aircraft. It was not without confusion in many people's minds before they became used to the changes. For example, the Douglas F4D Skyray overnight became a F-6, while the F-110 McDonald Phantom II suddenly was the new F-4D, one more than twice as fast as the other! At this time the TV-2 was redesignated as the T-

An early TV-2 out of NAS Patuxent River, Maryland with its IFR hood closed for instrument training. -Conger

A TV-2 belonging to the US Naval Reserve at NAS Glenview, Illinois. The red band on the fuselage was for quick visual identification that the aircraft belonged to the reserves and was not regular USN. Useful information to other pilots and air traffic controllers, for one could never anticipate what a reservist was going to next with his aircraft, for sometimes they didn't know, either. -Balogh/Menard via Davis

T2V 144210, construction number 1114, from that largest batch of produced Sea Stars. A decidedly hump-backed profile. This aircraft bears the last paint scheme in use by the T2V. -Bremer via Esposito

T2V-1 144146 belonged to NAS Miramar, California and finished out its service life as a well-worn hack. -Kasulka via Esposito

33B, while the USAF version remained the T-33A, even though they were virtually identical. But, the T2J "Buckeye" became the T-2, while the T2V was the new T-1. Just another of McNamera's Folly's.

At the completion of the USAF's T-33A training program it was stated that over 36,000 pilots had been trained in the T-Bird. This was the highest number trained in a jet-type aircraft in the world. The North American Aviation AT-6 holds the record for training the highest number of pilots, while the Northrop T-38 is in contention for the T-33's record, but it will take it at least another decade to even come close! By 1970 the only Navy T-33Bs still in service were with their reserve units and utilized for proficiency and general hack service. Likewise, the USAF had relegated the T-Bird to similar roles in all commands except for the Air Defense Command that continued to fly it as a target ship. The 48th Fighter Interceptor Squadron still had fourteen T-33s in service in 1982, with one, 57-734, having amassed more than 7,000 flying hours. The T-Birds at Tyndall AFB were finally retired in the summer of 1988, and the last of the Air National Guard T-33s was retired in the fall of that year.

Of all the T-33s built, close to half—4,300 examples—were lost to one form of attrition or another.

Foreign Countries Flying the T-33

Belonging to Belgium, FT-29 (53-5753) was assigned to 11 Smaldeel in August 1973. -Centurion via Davis

FT-36 (55-3047) as assigned to Belgium's 11 Smaldeel. Belgium's T-33s were replaced by Alpha Jets in 1979. -Curtis

T-33As commenced to be transferred from the United States to foreign countries in 1952 under the Mutual Aid Defense Pact , MDAP. The first of these were to Belgium and France, with other allotments in various numbers to other member countries of the NATO alliance following throughout the decade. As time progressed, members of the Rio Pact countries were then included, along with shipments to other friendly governments. Then, as T-33s began to become surplus to USAF needs, as well as Canada and France, many more of their T-Birds were sold to other foreign countries. In all, over forty countries have or continue to operate the T-33 in one form or another.

Belgium: Belgium received thirty-eight T-33s between March 1952 and the end of 1956. These were operated in a training role by 11VZZ/Smaldeel and 31 Smaldeel. In 1962 six T-33s were loaned to Holland for use in a joint training program, and supplemented by two more in 1965/66, with seven surviving T-33s being returned in 1972. The remaining T-33s were scheduled for replacement by Alpha Jets in 1979.

Bolivia: Fuerza Aerea Boliviana. Received thirteen Canadian built T-33A/Ns (Mk.3s, identified as CL-30s) in 1973, which were serialed as FAB 600/612. At least three of these were lost by 1977. In 1978 they received five more CL-30s, which were then serialed FAB 615/619. These later CL-30s

Several surplus French T-33s were sold to Bolivia and confusion reigns as to their positive identity. These examples were either original Lockheed or Canadair production, and some may have been modified by France to their T-33SF version, and then they were given civilian registration identifications for ferry purposes. F-ZVLI is listed as being both ex RCAF 21042 and 21247, so the registration may have been used more than once! -Isham

T-33A 14675 was ex USAF 50-429. It crashed in Canada. -Canadair

21627. Notice that the National Insignia has been deleted on the underside of the wings, and how the anti-glare black on the tip tanks does not completely cover the inside portion of the tanks. Also, the roll-down of the IFR hood does not conform to USAF standards. -Lockheed

were assigned to the Grupo Aereo Misto at Cochabamba to replace AT-6s. In 1985 FAB received eighteen more T-33As surplus from France. At the end of 1997 Bolivia was believed to still possess seven AT-33As and eleven T-33As.

Brazil: Forca Aerea Brasileira. The largest country in South America received a combination of F-80Cs and fifty-eight AT/ T-33As in the late 1950s. The T-33As were identified as FT-33s, for fighter/trainers, and utilized the two .50 caliber nose machine guns. They were serialed in the FAB as 4310/4367. In 1967 five more AT-33As were received, and they replaced the Meteors then in use. These AT-33A-20s served in multi-function roles of both tactical and training until they began to be withdrawn in favor of the Embraer-built Aermacchi MB 326GB in April 1972. The T-33, itself, continued into mid 1975 when they were withdrawn from service in favor of more modern aircraft. They had been assigned to 1, 4 and 14 Grupo de Aviacao de Caca.

Burma: Union of Burma Air Force. In the 1960s the USAF supplied to Burma at least six AT-33As and an unknown number of T-33As. The AT-33As represented the UBAF's sole interceptor strength, while Siai Marchetti SF.260MBs were used in a COIN role, primarily to ferret out narcotics.

Canada: Royal Canadian Air Force. The RCAF received their first twenty T-33s in the form of a loan in May 1951, with deliveries continuing to January 1952, under Project AMC-3T-14. These T-Birds came from AF Contract Numbers AF 9205 and AF 14806 and became identified as T-33 Mk. 1s, "Silver Stars," and these were assigned RCAF Serial Numbers 14675/14694. They all had the then standard underslung type tip tanks. The last one furnished, 51-4198/ 14695, became the single T-33 Mk. 2 (Lockheed designated as the T-33A (N), with the "N" identifying it as Rolls Royce Nene powered), and it was the prototype for the future Canadair production T-33 Mk. 3.

A then envisioned requirement for ten more "on loan" T-33As brought 51-6713/-6717 and 51-6743/-6747 out of AF Contract 14086. These, apparently, did not receive RCAF serial numbers and retained standard USAF markings except for the Canadian Maple Leaf national insignia.

The T-33A (N)/ Mk. 2 example was first flown by Canadair pilot William Longhurst on December 22, 1952. Their Mk.2/ Mk.3 differed from the Lockheed version by the exchange of a Rolls Royce Nene 10 in lieu of the Allision J33-A-25, an engine which produced 500 pounds more thrust, along with minor cockpit revisions. The initial assignment of the "borrowed" Mk. 1s was to 416 Squadron, a Mustang squadron at

A Silver Star of 3 Advanced Flying School, Gimli, Manitoba. Modelers might note the angle of the deployed speed brakes and the protrusion of the tailpipe.

RCAF 133052, previously their 21052, photographed at Vancouver September 29, 1978. -Phillips

A splendid CT-133 of VU 33 with its modified nose for electronic emitters. It is bearing special markings in honor of 38 years of service. -Soulaine via Isham

The same CT-133 with standard markings. It was photographed at Tyndall AFB, Florida on October 25, 1982 during a William tell Gunnery & Rocketry meet. -Curry via Isham

133174 of 414 Squadron, the Black Knights, celebrating the squadron's 50th Anniversary. -Harrison via Isham

Trenton that was slated for conversion to Mk.2 Sabres (a Canadair license-built version of the North American Aviation F-86E), and to Canadair, who had expressed the interest in building the T-33 under license from Lockheed. Subsequent assignments were to RCAF squadrons at Chatham and St. Hubert. Of these borrowed T-33s, most of those that were not lost in accidents were returned to the USAF in 1953 for subsequent transfer to the Air National Guard, while the remainder were dispatched to Greece or Turkey under MDAP.

A contract for Canadian production of their Mk.3 version was signed in April 1952 to begin with Serial 21001, and the first example was rolled out in November. Production continued until March 1958, for a total of 656 examples, 21656 being the last produced. Of those produced, 21051/21199 corresponded to the T-33A-1 and carried the standard T-Bird armament system, while the remainder equated to the T-33A-5 instrument trainer. All the Silver Stars were later renumbered as 133001/133656 and reidentified as the CT-133. A

21280 of Canada's Armed Forces. The Canadian military force was undergoing a combination of consolidation and an identity crisis at the time, and wasn't quite sure how to identify themselves as the old RCAF was being renamed. -Centurion via Davis

133299 initially belonged to the RCAF's Overseas Ferry Unit, and later was assigned to 410 Squadron. -Curry via Isham

133315 during a visit to the Experimental Aircraft Association's annual airshow at Oshkosh, Wisconsin on July 29, 1984. -Phillips

A nice view of 21331. Notice that the under wing aircraft insignia and identification numbers are in both directions, for easy identification and to discourage unnecessary low flying. -Henry via Isham

A Silver Star, 21333 of 425 Squadron while visiting Westover AFB, New York on July 14, 1983. -Rrys via Isham

"Kiwi" of the 1st Canadian Air Group celebrating attaining 10, 000 hours total flying time on this Silver Star. -Wolley via Isham

number of these T-33s/CT-133s were transferred to foreign countries by the RCAF as they reduced their forces in Europe, notably to France and Turkey. (Those designated for export being identified as T-33A/Ns or CL-30s). The Royal Canadian Navy received their first Mk.3 Silver Stars in January 1955, and these were assigned to VT-40 at HMCS Shearwater to provide initial jet training for future Canadian F3H Banshee pilots. In 1959 VT-40 was absorbed into VU-32, also at Shearwater. F3H operations ceased in 1962, and after this time the RCN Silver Stars were relegated to serving as target tugs and simulated maritime aggressors. In 1968 when the Canadian armed forces were unified VU-33 at Comox on the west coast joined VU-32 in this role. The CT-133 served in a training role with the RCAF until June 1974, but it still re-

21441 with the bilingual identification system brought on by the French separatist influence in eastern Canada. -Williams

Another example of 414 Squadron Silver Star markings. photographed during a visit to MCAS El Toro, California on May 1, 1994. -Kaston via Isham

133450 at Royal Air Force Mildenhall in May 1991 just before the Canadian Silver Stars were withdrawn from overseas usage. -Curtis

Canada's version of the RT-33, 21557 belonged to 408 Squadron before being surplused and becoming N99175 on the U. S. civil scene. Note the revised nose configuration. -Isham

21574 of the Red Knight aerial demonstration team. It later became a display aircraft at the Canadian Aeronautical Collection, Rockcliffe, Ontario. -Davis

21577 renumbered as 133577 at Abbotsford August 12, 1978 with the bilingual identification system then in vogue. Verron -via Phillips

133579 of 434 squadron bearing special markings in 1993. -LeBaron via Isham

The latest, to date, Canadian Silver Star markings, which are overall two-tone gray. Even in their subtleness they are attractive. -Graser via Isham

21616/133616 of the Golden Hawks acrobatic team in its original scheme with the last two digits of its serial number repeated on its speed brakes. The Golden Hawks were a premier Sabre demonstration team. -MAP via Curtis

mains in active service within the RCAF. Five examples were modified to a RCAF version of the RT-33A with forward and vertical Vinten cameras that then served with 408 Squadron at Rockliffe, Ontario, and they served until April 1970 when the squadron was inactivated and the aircraft retired. Ten have been modified to ET-133 or EW-133 standards with DPT-1 threat transmitters in their noses, whereupon they can be utilized as electronic aggressors for training maritime air defense forces, being able to simulate Exocet or other missiles. Others are used for additional maritime support by the Maritime Command. And, as expected, the remaining are in general service as squadron "hacks," proficiency and navigational trainers by four dedicated squadrons attached to four Canadian fighter wings. Forty-five conventional CT-133s remained operational at the end of 1997, and as they are presently being upgraded with digital cockpits, it is forecasted that they will remain in service until at least 2005.

CT-133 21625 of 416 Squadron, based at Cold Lake, Alberta enjoying a warmer climate at Barksdale AFB, Louisiana during the 1982 Strategic Air Command Bomb Competition. -Sibert

Chile: Fuerza Aerea de Chile. Chile received their first four T-33As on October 18, 1956, from Marietta, Georgia. Four others were received in May 1964. Their original serial numbers were J-2x series, but were later reserialed in a J-3xx range. At least three RT-33s were also assigned. They were flown alongside of their F-80Cs in Grupo 12 at Punta Arenas. They were withdrawal from service in 1974, due to a lack of spare parts, and replaced by A-37s. J-317 is on display at Bahia Catalina.

Colombia: Fuerza Aerea Colombiana. Received six T-33As in 1954 as the first South American nation to receive jet air-

One of the first T-33As supplied to the Fuerza Aerea Colombiana in 1954. -Flightlines via Conger

An immaculate FAC T-33A/N. -Slowiak via Menard

DT-492 (51-17492), but still bearing the USAF style buzz numbers, and belonging to the Danish Air Force. It was photographed at Weathersfield Air Base, England in May 1959. -Gradidge via Olson

craft from the United States under the Reimbursable Assistance Program. These were supplemented by further T-33A/Ns, AT/T-33As and four RT-33As, for a total of at least 32 aircraft. The last twelve of these being delivered in 1978. Assigned serial numbers were in the FAC 20xx series. The primary use was that of trainers, with a secondary role of Counter Insurgency (COIN). Their primary base was at Germon Olana, and they were still active in 1993.

Cuba: Fuerza Aerea Ejercito de Cuba/Fuerza Aerea Revolucionaria. Between June 1954 and August 1956 the FAEC received eight T-33As from the United States, serialed FAEC 701, 703, 705, 707, 709, 711, 713 and 715. The first four were assigned to the "Tenth of March" Fighter Squadron at Campo Grande.

After Castro's overthrow of the Batista government, their air force incurred a name change, from the FAEC to the FAR, and the country's alignment was severed from the United States in favor of the USSR, and their FAR began to equip with Soviet produced aircraft.

During the Bay of Pigs fiasco their T-33s were active as interceptors and shot down five Douglas B-26s, two being flown by American crews. On April 17, 1961, FAR 711 was flown by Captain Alvaro Prendes, FAR 703 was flown by TTE Rafael del Pino, and FAR 935 (sic) by TTE Alberto Fernandez, each destroying a foreign flown B-26. On April 19 Captain Prendes in FAR #711 shot down one of the American flown B-26s, while Major Enrique Carreras-Rola in FAR 709 downed the other. (One of their T-33s, identification unknown, was lost on April 15, with its pilot, TTE Acosta, being killed. The cause was unknown).

Denmark: Kongelige Danske Flyvevaben (Royal Danish Air Force). Twenty-six T-33As were received altogether, with the first twelve arriving in 1953-54. These were assigned to Station Flight Karup. In 1956 this unit became "Traeningsflight," (Training Flight) for their F-84Gs based at Aalborg. The second batch, the fourteen further examples arrived between April and June 1961, and were assigned to the Traeningsflight, as well as individual air bases. In April 1966 the Traeningsflight

DT-728 was USAF 51-8728 and it was transferred to Denmark under MDAP as a part of their allotment of twenty-six examples. -Menard

After being assigned to Nellis AFB, Nevada, 51-4502 was flown to Boston, Massachusetts and prepared for a MDAP transfer to France, where it became 338-HD. It was later sold to Singapore as #901. Rankin -via Olson

55-3095 of 10 Esk, French Air Force. A T-33A delivered as a T-33A-US and later converted to a T-33SF. -Pelletier

51-17546 also belonged to 10 Escadre De Chase. -Pelletier

relocated to Skrydstrup and expanded to squadron size as the "Traeningeskadrille," (Training Squadron). This squadron was disbanded on December 31, 1974, and the T-33s disbursed to Station Flights. The T-33 remained in use until May 17, 1977, when the final one was retired at Karup.

Ecuador: Fuerza Aerea Ecuatoriana, aka Escuela de Aviacion Militar. A dozen T-33As were received at Guayaquil in 1962 as a part of the Rio Defense Pact, to be utilized in a training role. They were serialed in an AT-7xx and AT-9xx series. Initially, these were to be retired in 1976, which was postponed until circa early 1980s in favor of the BAe Strikemaster Mk.2. However, in 1988 the FAE obtained twenty-five more surplus USAF T-33As, which are believed to still be in service.

Ethiopia: Imperial Ethiopian Air Force. In 1959 the IEAF received twelve T-33As from the USAF. In 1960 these were followed by twenty T-33A/Ns from Canada, and then in 1974 they received two RT-33As. By 1979 eleven T-33s remained in service as trainers at Bishoftu, and all were believed to have been withdrawn from service by 1984.

A T-33SF of 10 Esk. There were no visible differences between the USAF, Canadair or French versions of the T-Bird. -Pelletier

France: Armee de l'Air. The Armee de l'Air flew a total of 224 T-33s, making them the fourth largest user of the type after the United States, Canada and Japan. Exactly where all of these specific aircraft came from is unknown, but they are known to have possessed at least sixty Lockheed production examples directly from MDAP allocations, as well as sixty more Canadair models.

The first T-33As were delivered to French Morroco on October 4, 1951, and assigned to the Meknes Fighter School.

RT-33A 33-XW (54-1543) of the FAF bearing the Cross of Lorraine on its nose. -Lockheed

A RT-33 of the Iranian Air Force at Shinuz in 1961. -Mayner via Curtis

9-31 (53-5795), a RT-33 from Italy resplendent in a high-visibility orange, which held up much better in the weather than the day glow paint. -Davis

The second batch were allotted to the Centre d 'Entrainement au vol sans visibilite (Roughly, Blind Flying School, ie: Instrument training). The third allotment was to the 13th All-Weather Fighter Wing's Section de vol sans visibilite in 1955. By the end of 1956 France had received a total of ninety-five T-33As, which they redesignated as T-33S-US, and six RT-33s.

In 1959 France received fifty-nine Silver Star Mk.3s from Canada under MDAP, and these were designated as T-33S-C to differentiate from the Lockheed examples. Further Lockheed T-33As were received under MDAP in 1964, 1966 and 1967. The last allocation came in the form of ten surplus T-33As from Norway in 1968-69.

In 1961 the second phase of pilot training had moved to Tours and assigned to Base-Ecole 705 to provide training in T-33As and Mystere IVAs, to provide pilots training to a total of seventy-five hours before they moved to more advanced aircraft. At this time the T-33s were already considered by the Armee de l'Air to be outmoded. In later years the majority of French T-33 pilot training was conducted by GE 314 Ecole de Chasse at Tours or by the Center d' Instruction squadron 328 at Bordeaux. Some additional training was by Escadron d' Entrainement 12/30 at Reims.

Also in 1961 the Armee de l'Air decided to convert their T-33S-US and T-33S-C to a common standard, as there had been noted problems with confusion between pilots flying the two different aircraft with different engines and instrumentation. Initially, one of each was modified. They received new Hispano Suiza license-built Nene engines, updated navigational equipment and radios, and new ejection seats and became identified as T-33SFs. The first flight test was accomplished in March 1961, and as it was successful, it was decided to go ahead and modify a further eighty-three examples, with the first of these being completed on April 7, 1964.

By 1978 fifty-eight T-33SFs/T-33S-USs remained in their inventory, but these were scheduled for replacement by the Dassault-Dornier Alpha Jet between 1978-1981. As the T-Birds were phased out, those furnished by the United States that had not been modified to T-33SF standards were returned to the USAF for disposal. Others were refurbished and delivered to other countries, such as Singapore in 1980, Turkey in 1981-83, Thailand in 1982, and Bolivia in 1985.

Greece: Elliniki Aeroporia (Hellenic Air Force). In 1972 Greece received 12 ex Luftwaffe T-33As, and 33 more in 1975. By 1979 360 Mira at Elefsis was flying a combination of T-33As and North American Aviation T-2E Buckeyes, with the T-33 in a phase-out mode. However, this action was curtailed, and forty-seven remained in service in 1997.

Guatemala: Fuerza Aerea Guatemalteca. Five T-33s were supplied in 1971. Based at Los Cipresales, they were assigned to Esquadron de Caza-Bombardeo for training. (1979). Known serial numbers were FAG 728, 735 and 749.

Honduras: Fuerza Aerea Hondurena. Three RT-33A based at San Pedro Sula for reconnaissance. Additional T-33s for training. (1979). Serial FAH 200 was known to be a T-33. All were later reserialed in the FAH 12xx sequence, but serial numbers for other examples are unknown.

Built in 1957, 71-5283 of the Japanese Air Self Defense Force at Iruma Air Base, Japan in January 1974. -Centurion via Davis

Previously USAF 53-5373, this T-33A-1LO was one of an initial batch transferred to the JASDF before Kawasaki was able to commence production of the T-Bird in Japan. -Johnson via Olson

A 1959 Kawasaki production T-33, as prefixed by the "91." Note the bilingual 'Beware of Blast' in front of the tailpipe. -Williams

Indonesia: Tentara Nasional Indonesia-Angkatan Udara (Indonesia Armed Forces-Air Force). In 1972 the USAF supplied a dozen T-33As to Indonesia after they signed an aid agreement with Australia. These T-33s were utilized in a training role at Halim until replaced by the BAe Hawk in the early 1980s.

Iran: Imperial Iranian Air Force. The IIAF became independent under their Ministry of War in August 1955. They received their initial nine RT/T-33As in 1956, which were assigned to their F-84G squadrons at Mehrabad. By 1961 the IIAF had nine T-33As and twelve RT-33s in service, with the RT-33s assigned to the 1st Tactical Reconnaissance Squadron at Mehrabad. By January 1965 the only IIAF combat units were the single squadron of RT-33As for reconnaissance and three squadrons of F-84Gs, (Which were to be replaced by 1967 with F-5s). By 1966 the 1st TRS was down to eleven RT-33s and three T-33As. In 1979 the twenty-five plus T-33s then known to belong to the IIAF were scheduled for replacement.

Iraq: It is believed that Iraq operated sixteen RT-33As circa 1970.

Italy: Aeronautica Militare Italiana. The AMI received their first T-33A in 1952 under MDAP, for a total of 75 examples. Then, in Fiscal Year 1954 15 RT-33As were accepted. The combination RT/T-33A served in all standard functions with the AMI. The Comando Scuole dell' AMI (Air Force Training Command) operated their advanced jet flying school at Foggia, and also their "Air University" at Amendola with T-33As until they were replaced by G.91Ts in 1964/65. In the mid 1960s the RT-33As were withdrawn from their reconnaissance role and utilized by the Reparto Radiomisure for flight checking radio and radar facilities. By 1979 they had only three remaining T-33s, which were assigned to 14 Stormo GE at Pratica di Mare.

Japan: Japanese Air Self-Defense Force, JASDF. The JASDF is the largest portion of a triad force—ground, air, and naval—that is the Japanese Defense Agency. In 1954 the newly

71-5283 of Kawasaki production in the landing flare late in its service life. It had been upgraded to T-33A-25 standards by having TACAN navigational equipment installed. -Lockheed

Out to pasture, ex USAF 51-5625 of the JASDF on display at the old Johnson Air Base, Japan. -Williams

52-9814 as possessed by the Libyan Arab Republic Air Force

created JASDF began receiving sixty-eight T-33As and some T-34As to commence training, and in December 1955 their first surplus USAF F-86Fs. In 1956 the JASDF received two T-33As from Lockheed Aircraft Services to serve as pattern aircraft for future construction. These were followed by eighteen more unassembled aircraft, which were then assembled by Kawasaki and serialed 51-5601/568. Following this, Kawasaki constructed 210 examples at their own plant. These were serialed 61-520, which began 1956 construction, 71-xxxx for 1957, 81-xxx for 1958, through 91-5410 for 1959 contracts. (Simultaneously, Mitsubishi commenced construction of the F-86 and Fuji the T-34 for JASDF use). In 1964 the JASDF began giving their aircraft names, as the T-33A became the Wakataka, "Young Hawk," for public relations purposes.

By 1979 186 JASDF T-33As remained in service as trainers assigned to 33 Squadron at Hamamatsu and 7 and 35 Squadrons at Matsushima. At the beginning of 1997 forty remained operational in a liaison role, but by the end of 1997 this number was reduced to just twenty.

Libya: Libyan Arab Republic Air Force. Formed as the Royal Libyan Air Force in 1959, the RLAF received two T-33s in August 1963, and an unknown number later, but after a military coup in 1969 the air force reformed as the Libyan Arab Republic Air Force and went to France for military supplies. (Pilot training was conducted in these T-33s at Wheelus Air Base under USAF supervision). After the Six Day War in 1973 the LARAF further aligned with Russia for supplies, and by 1979 operated a mixed bag of equipment supplied by Russia and France. By this time they were down to just three T-33s, operated in a training role from Zawia.

Mexico: Fuerza Aerea Mexicana. Fifteen T-33As beginning 1961 and numbering JE-001/015, assigned to 202 Esuadron Aereo Jet de Pelea at Satillo in a training role. In 1972 seven more were ordered through Consolidated Aero Export from Holland, hence "N" numbers were assigned, but delivery was never accomplished and they remained on the U.S. Civil Registary. In 1987 forty more were obtained from the USAF as they were withdrawn from active United States service.

M-37 of the Netherlands KLu. M-37 was 55-4950 from the second batch of T-33s supplied under MDAP. It was lost in a crash on June 10, 1971. -Menard

Out to pasture as a gate guard, M-5 was 51-9028, one of the first T-33s supplied to the KLu. -via Conger

W-DP of the Norwegian Air Force with what appears to be a flying beer bottle depicted on its fuselage. -via Curtis

One of the KLu's acrobatic team, "Whisky 4," T-33s at Deelen. -via Conger

Apparently thirty of these were modified to AT-33A standards with underwing .50 caliber machine gun pods. These were serialed JE-017/056 and were assigned to newly activated 210, 211 and 212 Esuadrons. At the end of 1997 thirty AT/T-33s were still operational.

Netherlands: Koninklijke Luchtmacht, KLu (Royal Netherlands Air Force). The first 36 KLu T-33s were delivered between August 1952 and October 1955. In 1956 three RT-33As were also supplied under MDAP, proceeding delivery of RF-84Fs. An additional five T-33As were delivered in 1957, while thirteen more were obtained in 1964/65. Eleven of these were purchased outright from surplus USAF stocks (Not MDAP), and two were obtained from Belgium. Five additional surplus airframes were obtained at the same time to be used for spare parts. Seven of the 1964/65 purchase were later sold to Mexico, being moved there via the United States, and receiving temporary civilian "N" numbers for ferry purposes.

The Netherlands was one of the few countries to fly the T-33 as an acrobatic demonstration aircraft, the team being known as the "Whisky Four."

The last operational flight of a KLu T-33 was on June 9, 1972. However, Dutch pilots continued to train with the type in Canada into the 1980s.

Nicaragua: Fuerza Aerea Nicaragua. Ten T-33As were delivered, with at least five being converted to AT-33As. They were based at Managua. Known serial numbers FAN-304 and -306. In 1981 the FAN changed their name to the Fuerza Aerea Sandinista, and at this time two or three examples were still operational.

Norway: Kongelige Norske Flyvapen, "Flyvapenet." Commencing in 1953 22 T-33As were supplied to Norway. Their primary assignment was to Skv. 718 (Squadron 718) at Sola, the Operational Training Unit. At Sola emphsis was on instru-

Norway only flew the T-33 for fifteen years, with their primary assignment being to Skv. 718 at Sola. -Menard

53-5639 of the Philippine Air Force at Clark Air Base December 4, 1956. All buttoned up against the rain. -Paul

57-679 of the Philippine Air Force. At this time conversion from F-51Ds to F-86s was complete as their primary mission aircraft. -Menard

ment and tactical training. They were phased out of service in 1968.

Paraguay: The small country of Paraguay is believed to possess six T-33As at the end of 1997.

Pakistan: (Royal) Pakistan Air Force. In 1947 Pakistan was created in two parts, East and West, separated by 1,100 miles of territory belonging to India. This odd arrangement continued until 1971 when East Pakistan became Bangladesh after a two-week war (Bangladesh obtained one T-33 and three Sabres after this conflict, which they flew until they were forced to ground them, due to a lack of spare parts). The "Royal" was dropped from their name on March 23, 1956, when it was recognized that Pakistan was an Islamic Republic. In the late 1950s the USAF began supplying T-33As, F-86Fs and B-57Bs to the RPAF, but such support ended after a war with India in 1965, and did not resume until the late 1970s. The first fifteen T-33s were delivered to 2 (Fighter Conversion) Squadron at Mauripur to replace Tempests and Furies. An additional six RT-33As were supplied at a later date, which were assigned to a Tactical Reconnaissance Flight. By 1979 the RPAF had a dozen T-33s remaining in a training role at Mauipur. By 1991 this number was reduced to nine that had been switched to use as target tugs, flown by B Flight, 2 Squadron, from Masroor. Two RT-33As and nine T-33As remain in service at the end of 1997.

Peru: Fuerza Aerea del Peru. The first six T-33As were delivered circa 1955 for use in a training role. It appears that by 1965 at least twenty-five T-33As were in service with the FAP. They were assigned to the Peruvian Air Academy, Academia del Aire, at Las Palmas, and also to Grupo de Caza 12 at Talara, a Hawker Hunter/F-86F unit. At least eight examples were modified to AT-33A standards and these were still in use in 1979.

Philippines: Philippines Air Force. Based at Nichols Air Base, the PAF received their first jet aircraft in 1957 in the form of F-86Fs and T-33As. The 105th Combat Crew Training Squad-

55-2257 at Clark Air Base late in its service life, after being painted in anti-corrosion gray. -Aindo via Menard

56-1602 of Forca Aerea Portuguesa. Ex USAF, it had come to them from the 10th TRW post 1966. -Magendie via Slowiak/Menard

FAP 1911 from the first batch of T-33As supplied in 1953. -via Conger

Another ex USAF T-33A, FAP 1920 was 56-1605. -Menard

ron, (Identified by the USAF method.) based at Basa Air Base is known to have operated at least a dozen T-33As and three or more RT-33s in 1981. After the USAF left the Philippines it is believed that several more examples were transferred to their service.

Portugal: Forca Aerea Portuguesa. The first jet propelled aircraft received by the FAP were the Lockheed T-33 and the de Havilland T.11 Vampire, which was obtained to compare against the T-Bird. The T-33 was selected as the winner, and fifteen were delivered in 1953, these serialed 1901/1915. Then five T-33A(N)s were received from Canada and three more from the USAF, and serialed 1917/1925, with a single RT-33 serialed 1916. A later assignment brought four more into their inventory, serialing 1951/1955. By 1979 they had a dozen T-33As remaining in training roles. (Portugal does not use squadron numbers, instead the units are identified by the base to which they are assigned. BA-5 at Monte Real and BA-1 at Sintra were the respective units).

Saudi Arabia: Royal Saudi Air Force. In 1957 the USAF supplied six T-33As (along with ten F-86Fs) under MDAP to modernize the RSAF. These were operated by 15 Squadron at Dhahran until replaced by F-5Fs, (Similar to the two-seat T-38, but capable of doubling as a tactical aircraft.) in 1976.

Singapore: In 1980 at least thirteen ex French Air Force T-33SFs were transferred to the SADC, to be serialed in the 9xx range. At least half of these were assigned French civilian registry identifications in the F-BJDA and F-BKVA series during their transfer.

South Korea: Republic of Korea Air Force, ROKAF. The ROKAF began receiving T-33As in in 1956, along with surplus USAF F-86Fs, and then F-86Ds. Modernization continued with F-5s supplied in the 1960s, F-4Es in the 1970s and F-16s in the 1980s. Initially, by 1959, the ROKAF had up to thirty T-33A assigned to two training squadrons, however by 1962 there was just the 16th Basic Flying Training Squadron

A T-33A from the second batch transferred to the FAP, but its serial number is unknown. -Menard

56-1629 as supplied to the Republic of Korea Air Force, ROKAF. The tail markings are a carry-over from the 58th FBW. -Aindo via Menard

Another view of ROKAF 56-1629. Age and photographic processing have weakened the images reds. -USAF via Menard

54-1590 of the ROKAF with fluorescent tip tanks. It was assigned to the ROKAF 10th Fighter Wing at Suwon Air Base, South Korea in 1968. -S. H. Miller via Menard

in operation at Taegu. In 1979 eighty T-33As remained in ROKAF service for jet conversion training and other purposes, and by the end of 1997 twenty-five were still operational.

Spain: Ejercito del Aire. Spain redesignated their T-33s as E.15s. The first six of a total of fifty-eight examples arrived in Spain on March 24, 1954, and was assigned to Escuela de Reactores. Later examples were assigned to Grupo 41 and Escuela 102, 104 and 201. There last E.15 was not retired until after 1980.

Taiwan: Chinese Nationalist Air Force. Exact figures on T-33 deliveries to Taiwan (Formosa) are unknown. Deliveries began in 1953 at the cessation of the Korean Conflict with the transfer of surplus USAF Far East Air Forces T-33s and F-84Gs. The T-33s were utilized for advanced training after the T-6 and T-28, until they were replaced by T-38s.

Thailand: Royal Thai Air Force. The RTAF began receiving F-84Gs and T-33As in 1957 to supplement their 200 F8Fs and armed T-6s. (The Bearcats were replaced in 1962, yet the T-6s were still active in 1979). 11 Squadron, 1st Wing, at Don Muang was the prime operator of the RT/T-33 in RTAF service, having four of the previous and 20 of the latter still active in a training capacity in 1979. In 1982 the RTAF received some T-33SFs from France, bearing civilian registry letters in the F-GBEA series for ferry purposes.By the end of 1997 three of the RT-33As and four T-33As were still in use by the RTAF.

Turkey: Turk Hava Kuvvetleri. By 1979 the THK had thirty T-33As remaining in their inventory for advanced training between T-37s and F-104s. Based at Cigli/Mizir, they were operated by the Hava Egitim Komutanligi (Air Training Command), 121 Filo. RT-33s were assigned to 113 Filo at Eskisehir, a composite unit also flying RF-84Fs with their 1st Tactical Air Force and these remained in use until October 29, 1980. Other supporting units had T-33As for liaison and other functions. In 1996 seventy-five RT-33As/T-33As were still reported as operational, but these were scheduled for withdrawal by the end of that year and are believed to have been withdrawn completely by the end of 1997.

Belonging to Ejercito del Aire, E15-52 was ex USAF 53-4993. In 1980 it was assigned to Grupo 41 at Avila, Spain. -Menard

Chinese Nationalist Air Force #3084. -Morris via Menard

CNAF #3311, ex USAF 56-1618. -Steinemann via Menard

A Royal Thai Air Force T-33A. Its actual identification is unknown. -Centurion via Davis

Uruguay: Fuerza Aerea Uruguaya. Eight AT/T-33As assigned to Brigaga 1, Grupo 1 at Carrasco (1979) for use as fighter-bombers. Numbered in a FAU-201/208 series. Two additional T-33s were also received to be used for spare parts, which were unserialed. At the end of 1997 five were believed to remain operational.

West Germany: The Luftwaffe was reestablished in 1956 with initial assignments of T-33As and RF/F-84Fs. They received a total of 192 T-33s, but began a replacement/phase-out of them in 1972, which was completed by 1980 with the Waffenschule 50 at Furstenfeldbruck being their last operator. The T-33A had been initially utilized at their advanced, "B" School at Furstenfeldbruck to provide eighty hours of training between the Piper Super Cub/Fouga Magister "A" School

An AT-33A of the FAU at Durazno in March 1990 celebrating the FAU's 77th Anniversary. -Smith

53-5772 as assigned to the Luftwaffe as their BD-796. All of the fuselage instruction stencils are bilingual German and English. Gradidge via Olson

Luftwaffe 9484, whose origin is unconfirmed. Its anti collision fluorescent paint is beginning to fade, as it did not hold up well in climatic conditions. -Centurion via Davis

and later Operational Training. -From October 1964 pilots selected for jet training would be taught in the United States.

Yugoslavia: Yugoslavia considered itself to be fiercely independent from both Eastern and Western political policies—even though it was an Eastern Block country it was independent of the Warsaw Pact.

The first JAF T-33s were delivered to Batajnica on March 10, 1953, and by the end of 1956 they had received twenty-four T-33As and twenty-one RT-33s. These were followed by fifty-four surplus U.S. Navy TV-2s in the early 1960s.

Initially, JAF jet pilots were trained in West Germany by the USAF prior to transitioning to the 200 F-84Gs supplied by the USAF. But by 1964 T-33As were also assigned to Plesco, Cerklje, Skopje, Titograd and Tuzla. Additionally, twenty-five were in use at Pula in an unknown capacity, while the RT-33s were based at Tuzla.

In 1976 further T-33As were received from Belgium and the USAF. However, in the 1960s the JAF had commenced purchasing Soviet aircraft and missiles, and then commenced building their own combat aircraft.

By 1979 the JAF RT-33s were still reported to be operational, and by 1980 their T-33As converted to "Tegliac's (Tugboats) and then designated as TT-33As were supposedly withdrawn. However it is thought that some may still survive in the countries of the former Yugoslavia.

One of the last foreign deliveries of new T-33s under MDAP was 58-595 to the Luftwaffe as their #9496, JB-395, as assigned to J. G. 72. -Menard

USAF Service by Stateside Command

Strategic Air Command

50-412 belonged to the 4025th Strategic Reconnaissance Wing at Laughlin AFB, Texas. For some reason the first digit of its serial number was changed from a 5 to a 0. Previously it had belonged to the 3645th Fighter Training Wing, also at Laughlin. -Williams

53-5993 at March AFB, California with SAC's "Milky Way" fuselage band. March was Headquarters 15th Air Force and the home of SAC's 22nd Bomb Wing. -Kasulka via Esposito

51-4309 as assigned to an unknown SAC unit. Their Milky Way fuselage band was the only remarkable item on their T-Birds. It was later donated to the Chicago, Illinois public school system as N8683E. -Paul

Military Air Transport Service/Military Airlift Command

52-9852 as assigned to the Military Air Transport Service at McGuire AFB, New Jersey. McGuire was the home of the 1611th Air Transport Wing, which became the 438th Air Base Group on January 8, 1966 when MATS was renamed as the Military Airlift Command. -Esposito

After previous assignments to the 127th Pilot Training Wing at Luke AFB, Arizona and then the 3555th PTW at Perrin AFB, Texas 50-415 was assigned to the 1611th ATW at McGuire AFB. -Esposito

Another T-33A-1LO of the 1611th ATW, this time on display at NAS Lakehurst, New Jersey. These T-Birds were primarily utilized for pilot proficiency by MATS pilots, who in those days were permitted to maintain currency in more than one type aircraft. -Esposito

A major sub-command of MATS was the Air & Airways Communications Service, AACS. In 1961 AACS was renamed as the Air Force Communications Service, AFCS, and then in 1979 expanded to become its own command as the Air Force Communications Command. Headquartered at Scott AFB, Illinois, (Along with Hq. MATS/MAC.) these AFCS T-Birds have some of the most attractive markings ever applied to USAF T-33s. -USAF via Leonard

An AFCS T-33 undergoing maintenance in the "peapatch" area at Scott AFB. Note the canopy latches silhouetted against the sky. These T-Birds were utilized for flight checking high altitude navigational aids, as USAF VORs and TACANs for certification for use in jet penetrations. -USAF via Leonard

MATS became the Military Airlift Command on January 1, 1966, with an according change in aircraft tail stripe markings. When this T-Bird was phased out of MAC service it was transferred to the 95th FITS. -Williams

58-631 of MAC's 63rd Military Airlift Wing, Norton AFB, California. Then flying C-141s, the 63rd MAW is noted for their participation in Operation Homecoming when they airlifted home former Vietcong POWs, as well evacuating south Vietnam refugees to the United States under operation New Life. -Williams

58-636 of MAC with a travel pod attached. It was later donated to the Warren High School, Waukegan, Illinois and registered as N83737. -Williams

Tactical Air Command

51-8569 belonged to the 479th Fighter Day Group at George AFB, California. The 479th flew a succession of F-51Ds, F-86Fs, F-100s and F-104s during their T-33 era. They were the replacement unit for the Korean War activated 131st Fighter Bomber Wing,an activated Air National Guard unit from Illinois and Missouri. -via Hansen

53-5218 at George AFB. The Airman Third Class on the T-Bird's wing is wearing a bush jacket uniform that was introduced in 1958 and abolished in 1962. It even came with a pith helmet! It was distinctively an unmilitary embarrassment. -Kasulka via Esposito

49-883 as assigned to the 56th Fighter Group at Selfridge AFB, Michigan on April 6, 1949. It bears the national flags of all the countries visited by the 56th FG during their first Fox Able mission. In May 1949 the 56th FG commenced Fox Able 2 to Furstenfeldbruck Air Base, Germany, delivering this T-Bird and three others, along with eleven F-80s, to the 36th Fighter Bomber Wing. This was the first mass delivery of jet aircraft by air to an overseas USAF unit. -McLaren collection

With its wing tip tanks painted gray, as well as its undersides, 52-9458 is pristine on the ramp at Nellis AFB, Nevada. The red streamer over the tip tank is attached to a safety pin to prevent an accidental dropping of the tank. -Williams

An AT-33A belonging to the 4430th Combat Crew Training Squadron, 4554th Combat Crew Training Wing, Myrtle Beach AFB, South Carolina. Note the underwing bomb ejector racks. The unit was responsible for training both TAC and foreign pilots in tactical AT-33 operations. -Larsen/Remington via Isham

A T-33A of the 4430th CCTS "Teeny Tigers." -Isham

53-6041 of the 27th Tactical Fighter Wing in 1969. Based at Cannon AFB, New Mexico, the main 27th TFW was just converting from F-100s to F-111s at the time of the photograph, but also operated some AT-33As. -Williams

53-5922, a T-33A-5 assigned to the 354th Combat Support Group, 354th Tactical Fighter Wing, Myrtle Beach, South Carolina. -Williams

Air Defense Command

The Air Defense Command was the largest USAF user of the T-33 beyond the Air Training Command. This was a necessity born of their mission, and the T-Bird was their "jack of all trades." It initial primary use was in instrument training, certification or requalification of their interceptor pilots, who by their very specialized mission had to be exceptionally proficient in instrument flying, for they never knew when or in what weather conditions they would be scrambled against an unknown target. As time progressed, their T-33s were utilized as target tugs during live firing exercises, as well as target ships during Faker Missions when they carried both electronic and manual radar jamming equipment to represent hostile aircraft attacking American targets.

56-1668 belonged to the 71st FIS, 28th Air Division at Malmstorm AFB, Montana. -Paul

The author's favorite. A "Dropkick" (Their radio callsign.) T-Bird belonging to the 85th Fighter Interceptor Squadron, Scott AFB, Illinois. As with most Air Defense Command Fighter Interceptor Squadrons, the 85th FIS originally had four T-33s, each identified by the symbol from a suite of cards. One crashed during a JATO takeoff killing the non-pilot riding in the back seat. Another exploded on takeoff, due to a fuel siphon into the plenum chamber, killing both pilots. 53-5078 survived to become a display aircraft at Dickinson, North Dakota. -Larkins via Menard

"Siouxlander IV", 51-8786, this T-Bird belonged to the Sioux City, Iowa Air Defense Sector. It later became a display aircraft at Bad Axe, Michigan. -Isham

"Siouxlander V" also belonged to the Sioux City ADS. Accepted by the USAF on June 25, 1952 under Project TRC-27T-407, it originally served with the 3520th Combat Crew Training Wing at Wichita AFB, Kansas. It later became a display aircraft at Orrville, Ohio. -Slowiak via Isham

"Siouxlander I" with the commanding colonel's eagle on its ventral strake. -Paul

52-9571 of the 4711th Air Defense Wing at Presque Isle AFB, Maine. It later became an AT-33 and was reassigned to TAC. -Paul

In totally non-remarkable markings 49-936 was assigned to the 33rd Air Base Group in support for the 33rd FIW on November 14, 1949. Photographed on May 21, 1950 at Otis AFB, Massachusetts. It later was transferred to O'Hare Field, Illinois and assigned to the 62nd FIS. Eventually it went to Moody AFB,Georgia and assigned to the 3550th Pilot Training Wing, to train future Air Defense Command interceptor pilots. It was lost in a crash on August 19, 1952. -Shipp via Olson

Also with chaff dispensers, 58-614 of the 328th Fighter Interceptor Wing at Richards-Gebaur AFB, Missouri. The 328th FIW was assigned to the 30th Air Division between April 1, 1966 and July 7, 1968,flying F-102As and later F-106As. -Geer via Isham

57-769 after previous assignment to the Luftwaffe as DA-399. This T-Bird flew under the radio callsign of "Scranton," being used by headquarters ADC to conduct Operational Readiness Inspections, ORI's, of their interceptor squadrons. -via Slowiak/Isham

"Jaws," 58-540, belonged to the 57th Fighter Interceptor Squadron at Keflavick Air Base, Iceland. Captured on liftoff on a practice intercept mission. -Sveinsson via Williams

Another view of "Jaws" on the ramp at Keflavick with an Electronic Counter Measures, ECM, pod under its wing. -Sveinsson via Williams

57-592 of the 57th FIS with a modified version of their squadron insignia depicted. All of the ancillary equipment to support a T-33 mission is present, and it must have been one of those proverbial "Rare days in June" to have such clear weather conditions. -Sveinsson via Williams

And who's afraid of the big bad Bear (TU-142). It was intercepted on July 10, 1979 by a 57th FIS T-Bird flown by Doug Barbier. -Barbier via Isham

57-592 of the 57th FIS leads a F4B of VMFA-115 off Iceland at the start of a practice interception mission. -Barbier via Isham

Moving across the top of the world to Alaska, we now have T-33As of the 21st Special Operations Squadron at Elmendorf AFB. They also carried "Arctic markings" to enhance discovery if they went down in hostile terrain. -Isham

Another 21st Composite Wing T-33A "in the flare" on final approach to Elmendorf AFB.

Outfitted with a pair of chaff dispensers and a radar reflector pod, (Identical in appearance to the travel pod.) to enhance its radar image, this T-33A belonged to the 5021st Tactical Operations Squadron, 21st Composite Wing, Elmendorf AFB, Alaska. -USAF

A pair of 21st SOS T-Birds prepare for takeoff from Elmendorf AFB, Alaska. -Brown via Isham

Up at Ladd Field, Fairbanks, Alaska in the early 1950s was the 449th Fighter Interceptor Squadron. 51-6650 was assigned to them on April 27, 1953, and later was transferred to the 18th FIS, also at Ladd. -Hafluer/ Homme via Isham

Bearing special Bicentennial markings, this T-Bird, 57-761, belonged to the 21st SOS at Elmendorf AFB. -Isham

Back across the northern wilds to Goose Bay, Labrador, 55-4401 belonged to the 59th FIS in 1966. At this time the squadron was flying F-102As. It has underwing pylons for chaff tanks. -Stewart via Isham

T-33A 51-4281 belonged to the 74th FIS at Thule Air Base, Greenland. The squadron was assigned to the North East Air Command in August 1954 from Presque Isle AFB, Maine with F-94s, converted to F-89s at Thule, and inactivated in June 1958. -O'neal via Isham

57-715 belonged to the 60th FIS at Otis AFB, Massachusetts. The 60th FIS was the first ADC squadron to obtain F-101Bs, in 1959. The squadron was inactivated in 1971. -Morris via Isham

57-592, also of the 60th FIS and with a minor variation to their paint scheme. Standard ADC practice was to place the squadron insignia on the port side of the vertical fin, ADC's insignia on the starboard side. The ADC insignia, itself, was a Walt Disney Studio creation. -Williams

57-767 of the 84th FIS. (Someone got carried away with the stencil machine and created a bogus serial number). It is carrying an ECM pod on its port pylon. -via Isham

58-672 belonged to the 460th FIS at Grand Forks AFB, North Dakota. The squadron was based there from April 1971 until they were inactivated in July 1974. Their primary mission aircraft had been the F-106A. -Waller via Isham

57-769 was assigned to Headquarters ADC at Colorado Springs, Colorado. The day-glow painted areas had originally been white, but were repainted in the anti-collision campaign that started in 1958. They flew under the radio callsign of "Scranton" and conducted the Operational Readiness Inspections. ORI's, of ADC interceptor squadrons. -Isham

In September 1968 the 11th FIS at Duluth, Minnesota was redesignated as the 87th FIS, while continuing to fly F-106As as their mission aircraft. -Rogers via Isham

An 11th FIS T-33A. Subservient to the Duluth Air Defense Sector, the squadron flew from the Duluth airport as a joint-use airfield until the based squadrons were inactivated or relocated and the facilities turned over to the city and state. -Jefferies via Isham

The 2nd FIS at McGuire AFB, New Jersey was one of the Air Defense Command's oldest squadrons, having started with P-61s in 1947. They converted to F-82s in 1948, which were followed by F-94As, F-84Gs and F-86Ds while based at McGuire. -Jefferies via Isham

The 5th FIS was another of the original 52nd Fighter Interceptor Group's squadrons. First at Mitchell AFB, Long Island, New York with the 2nd FIS, they also later moved to McGuire. In 1960 they relocated to Minot AFB, Montana (But this photograph was taken at Colorado Springs, Colorado). -Malerba via Isham

In September 1968 the 438th FIS at Griffiss AFB was redesignated as the 49th FIS and flew F-106As. Their T-Birds now have additional anti-collision lights installed on their lower fuselages. -Isham

A nice formation shot of 27th FIS T-33s of the 27th FIS out of Griffiss AFB, New York. At the time of the photograph they were flying F-94Cs. The tail band insignia was that of their parent 47th Air Defense Wing. -Ochmanowicz via Green/Isham

T-33A 51-6617 of the 18th FIS, 478th Fighter Interceptor Wing, Grand Forks AFB, Montana. It had originally been delivered to the USAF on July 2, 1952 with an initial assignment to the 3560th PTW at Webb AFB, Texas. -Stewart via Isham

Down in the rough at Ladd Air Force Base, Alaska in December 1957. 51-6650 had just been left behind at Ladd by the 18th FIS after that squadron had returned to the "lower forty-eight" when it truly got broken and bent. -via Menard

56-3670 belonged to the 48th FIS at Langley AFB, Virginia. Their mission aircraft had been F-102As until 1960, and then F-106As. -Strandberg via Isham

Belonging to the Bangor Air Defense Sector, 53-5979 was later donated to the University of Illinois at Champaign and registered as N4698T. It is now a gate guard at Willard Airport, Savoy, Illinois. -Slowiak via Isham

A 319th FIS T-33 taxies-in during William Tell 1963 at Tyndall AFB, Florida. Based at Homestead AFB, Florida, the 319th was ADC's last F-104 squadron. They were also the only ADC squadron to have earned kills during the Korean War while assigned to FEAF and flying F-94s. -Isham

A quartet of 318th FIS T-33As near McChord AFB. In the 1970s ADC began painting their T-Birds in "ADC gray" for corrosion control. -Dorr

A 318th FIS T-33A at McChord AFB, Washington. The "A" pennant on the vertical fin was a hard earned award for excellence in the air defense mission. -Larson/Remington via Isham

T-33A 56-1712 of the 95th FIS at Dover AFB, Delaware. "Mr. Bones" was their moniker for their insignia. They were a F-102 and F-106 squadron that had been inactivated in January 1973, only to be reactivated as the 95th Fighter Interceptor Training Squadron at Tyndall AFB in September 1974. -Morris via Isham

58-2098 was from the final batch of T-33A-5s produced. By this time the mass pilot training program fostered by the Korean War had long since passed and contracted for T-Birds were all assigned to non Air Training Command units. Note that the inside of the flaps of this 95th FIS T-Bird have been painted insignia red. -Hughes via Williams

A colorful but simple paint scheme on this T-33 of the 84th FIS at Hamilton AFB, California. Based there until 1968, the 84th then moved to Castle AFB, California and when their T-Birds were phased out, this example was donated to the Castle AFB Museum. -Pelletier

57-586 of the 87th FIS with lackluster markings. The 87th FIS had been inactivated at Lockburne AFB, Ohio in July 1968 only to be reactivated in September to replace the 11th FIS at Duluth. In may 1977 they moved to K. I. Sawyer AFB, Michigan. Both the squadron and the base have since been inactivated in the Air Force draw down. -Williams

57-606 belonged to the 21st Air Division, headquartered at McGuire AFB, New Jersey. The 21st AD was activated on April 1, 1966 and discontinued on December 31, 1967, only to be reactivated at Hancock AFB, New York on November 1969. -Williams

53-4897 of the 414th Fighter Interceptor Group at Oxnard AFB, California. The 414th FIG was the parent unit for the 437th FIS. Note that the lower half of the fuselage is painted gray. It became a display aircraft at Fall River, Wisconsin. -Slowiak via Isham

51-9078 of the 95th Fighter Interceptor Training Squadron at Tyndall AFB, Florida with chaff dispensers attached. Chaff was cut to specific lengths to jam specific radar frequencies, but it was a bit of a pathetic joke as it streamed out behind the dispensing aircraft and pointed like an arrow to exactly where the aircraft was. -Lockheed

58-577 of the 95th FITS at Tyndall. Behind the nose wheel doors is the TACAN antenna. -Lockheed

A line up of visiting T-33s at Tyndall AFB, Florida during William Tell 1963. The Mustang belonged to R. A. "Bob" Hoover, the noted acrobatic pilot who just retired his Mustang exhibition routine in 1997. -Isham

A 95th FITS T-33 at Tyndall after the squadron's reactivation in September 1974. They became the largest user of ADC T-Birds at this time. -Morris via Isham

April 1988 and the T-Bird approaches its final years as a mission aircraft with the 95th FITS, appropriately silhouetted against the setting sun off the Florida coast. -McLeod via Dorr

The Air National Guard and Air Force Reserve

The Air National Guard, ANG, and Air Force Reserve, AFRES, forces were another major user of the T-33. This was particularly the case with the ANG who began flying the T-33 in 1953 and continued with the type for another three decades with each ANG squadron possessing at least one example at one time or another. The AFRES, on the other hand, also began receiving T-33s in 1953, but only flew them in their few dedicated fighter squadrons until 1957 when those squadrons changed roles and the AFRES ceased tactical flying operations altogether for the next twenty years. When they resumed flying fighters once again in the 1970s, T-33s were furnished once again, but only in limited numbers.

55-4365 assigned to the AFRES at Mecham Field, Ft. Worth, Texas. The 2596th Air Reserve Flying Center, headquartered at Hensley Naval Air Station, Dallas, was the parent unit for the 448th Fighter Bomber Wing, which included the 711th Fighter Bomber Squadron. The 711th FBS, itself, flew a succession of F-80s, F-84s, and commenced training in F-86Hs before they were inactivated in October 1957. -Paul

A T-33A of the 349th Fighter Bomber Wing, 2346th AFRES Flying Center, Hamilton AFB, California. The 349th FBW was composed of the 312th, 313th and 314th Fighter Bomber Squadrons and was the largest AFRES flying unit during their F-51D, F-80C and post 1957 C-46 era. -via Esposito

A mixed bag of 349th FBW T-33s and F-80Cs with red and white tail stripes and tip tank markings. -via Esposito

58-503 as assigned to the 8401st Air Reserve Unit, Wright Patterson AFB, Ohio, but bearing the markings of the AFLC. It later was transferred to the 354th Tactical Fighter Wing. -Lockheed

52-9692 belonged to the 101st Fighter Interceptor Squadron at Otis AFB in 1982. At this time they were flying F-106s, but now they have F-15s. -Isham

52-9865, also from the 101st FIS. The squadron's lineage goes back to August 1917. At the time of this photograph, May 1954, the 101st had just received this T-Bird to facilitate transition to the F-94 that they would begin receiving the following month. -Paulsen via Taylor/Dorr

T-33A 53-4900 of Tennessee's 105th Tactical Reconnaissance Squadron at McGhee-Tyson AFB, Knoxville. The "Old Hickory Squadron" was flying RF-80s at the time. -Brown via Isham

The same 105th T-33A after a slight change in markings when the National Guard Bureau dropped the "ANG" in favor of "Air Guard" in the spring of 1961. The 105th switched roles and converted from RF-84Fs to C-97Gs and became an Air Transport Squadron. With the need for jet proficiency behind them, this T-Bird was transferred to the 5021st Tactical operations Squadron in Alaska. -Kasulka via Esposito

A pair of T-33As and F-86Es in the process of being transferred to Michigan's 107th FIS, with the Sabres replacing their old Mustangs and the T-Birds replacing their T-6Gs. T-33A 52-8671 is also listed as later being sent to Holland as their M-58 and to Ethiopia as their number 214. -USAF

52-9403 of Michigan's 107th FIS at Boise, Idaho and bearing a combination of both USAF and ANG markings while serving as a target towship. The squadron was in the process of switching from F-86Es to F-89Cs at the time of the photograph. -Paulson via Isham

53-4903 had originally been assigned to the Illinois 168th FIS at O'Hare Field, but when that squadron was inactivated in 1958 it was reassigned to the 108th FIS, also at O'Hare. The black rectangles below the aft fuselage are positioning points for the maintenance dolly. It became a display aircraft at Madison, Wisconsin. -Stevens

Bearing the Golden Gopher motif of the 109th FIS at Wold-Chamberlin Airport, Minneapolis, 52-9806 had one of the most distinctive ANG paint schemes during the squadron's F-51D and F-94A eras. -Coombs via Olson

For some reason the wonderful paint scheme originally on 52-9806 was removed by 1959 and it became a "plain Jane." Note the target towing apparatus under the port wing. When the 109th FIS converted to C-97s this T-Bird was MDAP'd to the Philippine Air Force. -Coombs via Olson

51-6808 with a pristine factory-fresh but plain paint scheme. It had just been delivered to the 110th Fighter Bomber Squadron, 131st Fighter Bomber Group at George AFB, California on August 23, 1952 for jet pilot proficiency. The Group was an activated ANG unit from Missouri and Illinois at the time and they were flying F-51Ds as their mission aircraft. When the 131st FBG returned to State Control in October this T-Bird was transferred to the 50th FBW at Clovis AFB, New Mexico. -Sommerich via Olson

56-1740 of "Lindbergh's Own" at Robertson Air National Guard Base, Lambert Field, St. Louis, Missouri. The 110th FBS received this example from New York's 139th FIS, and later transferred it to Nebraska's 173rd TRS. -Geer via Isham

52-9667 belonged to the 116th FIS, Washington ANG at the time of the photograph. The placement of their squadron insignia on the tip tanks is unusual. -Isham

Fantastically beautiful markings applied to a 111th FIS T-33 at Ellington Air National Guard Station. The 111th was running the ANG jet pilot instrument school at the time, as well as maintaining an ADC commitment. -Leader via Isham

A 119th FIS T-33 on takeoff from Atlantic City, New Jersey on a practice interception mission with a chaff dispenser under its port wing. Note that the inside of the flaps are painted insignia red. -Soulaine via Isham

58-611 of the 119th FIS at Atlantic City, New Jersey with the last markings applied to their squadron T-33s, which corresponded to those applied to their F-106As. The markings have often been confused with those applied to US Navy aircraft because of their style. -Phillips

50-401 was assigned to the 121st Fighter Bomber Squadron on July 6, 1953. It is being inspected by the D. C. Commissioners during the squadron's summer encampment at Travis Field, Georgia in 1955. (This Travis Field is not to be confused with Travis AFB, California). It was later assigned to the 111th FIS at Ellington ANGS, Texas and was written off in a belly landing. -Smith

Assigned to Headquarters National Guard Bureau, their T-Birds were maintained by the 113th Fighter Wing at Andrews AFB, Maryland, the parent unit for the 121st Fighter squadron. Note the generals stars on the ventral fin. -Isham

Assigned to Detachment 1, National Guard Bureau. The under fuselage travel pod was just the right size to hold the ubiquitous B-4 garment bag. -Lockheed

With an anti-collision fluorescent paint scheme, this T-33A belonged to Connecticut's 118th FIS. They converted from F-94Bs to F-86Hs in 1957 and became a Tactical Fighter Squadron. -Picciani via Isham

53-5943 of Oregon's 123rd FIS, 142nd FIG at Portland. The 123rd FIS was the ANG's last squadron to fly the T-Bird, and this example bears the last paint scheme to be utilized on the type. -Soulaine via Isham

48-365, one of the first T-33As, was assigned to Iowa's 124th Fighter Bomber squadron on June 10, 1953, just after the squadron was released from their Korean War activation and their return to Des Moines from Dow AFB, Maine. At this time they began conversion from F-51Ds to F-80Cs. -Iowa ANG via Olson

51-6745 of the 126th FIS at Billy Mitchell Field, Milwaukee, Wisconsin. This was one of the ex Royal Canadian Air Force T-33As, having served at North Bay, Ontario with 414 Squadron until its return to the USAF and assignment to the 126th on January 4, 1953. It eventually became a display aircraft at Huntington, Indiana. -Paul

All painted up for use as a target tug, 53-4904 belonged to the 126th FIS who were flying F-89Cs as their mission aircraft at the time. Air-to-air gunnery was (And still can be accomplished) in R-6903, a restricted flying area in the middle of Lake Michigan. This T-Bird was later assigned to the 179th FIS and on July 25, 1970 it ran off the runway, shearing its landing gear, and was written-off. -Stuckey via Olson

52-9542 of the Massachusetts ANG's 131st Tactical Fighter Squadron at Barnes Field, Westfield. The fin bands are red, and at the time of the photograph, the squadron's mission aircraft was the F-86H. She finished out her service life with California's 197th FIS. -Harrison via Paul

Vermont's 134th FIS, the "Green Mountain Boys," received 53-5121 from the Michigan ANG. -Isham

58-615 belonged to the 136th FIS at Niagara Falls, New York. The positioning of their squadron insignia is far further aft on the fuselage than usual. One wonders what the back seater is up to? -Taylor via Dorr

53-5393 of the Niagara Falls based 136th FIS in the last paint scheme applied to their T-Birds before they were phased out. -Rys via Isham

An unidentified T-Bird belonging to Delaware's 142nd FIS photographed during an early summer encampment. -Smith

53-5224 belonged to the 146th FIS, 112th FIG, Pennsylvania ANG. Based at Greater Pittsburgh. It later went to Texas's 111th FIS at Ellington ANGS for training future ANG T-33 pilots. -Woodo via Isham

52-9586 of Delaware's 142nd FIS at Newcastle. At the time of the photograph the 142nd was just beginning their conversion from F-51Hs to F-86As. In 1962 they became an air transport squadron and -9586 was sent to the Georgia ANG. It now resides with Southern Illinois University at Carbondale, Illinois as N49892. -Esposito

52-9800 "Over the fence" at Philadelphia, Pennsylvania in 1959. -Esposito

52-9401 as "Sam's Sedan" with a rare personal insignia on an ANG aircraft. It was also rare for the ANG to retain the "TR" buzz code on their aircraft. -Sommerich via Olson

52-9401 with slightly revised markings, of which the significance of the "Never fear a SAM is near." is unknown. -Dorr

56-3661 of Virginia's 149th TFS, who at the time were flying F-84Fs from Byrd Field, Sandston. It became an instructional airframe with the Detroit, Michigan High School system, being registered as N83615. -Hartman via Olmsted

53-5970 belonged to the 155th TRS at Memphis, Tennessee in 1961. The 155th switched roles and mission aircraft, converting from RF-84Fs to C-97As and became an air transport squadron later in the year. -Brown via Isham

53-6069 of the 157th FIS. Based at McEntire ANGB, their T-Birds bore excellent paint schemes. -Morris via Isham

T-33A 53-5901 of the 159th FIS at Jacksonville, Florida. The 159th has a long tradition of air defense missions and they were the first ANG squadron to win a William Tell gunnery and rocketry meet, with F-86Ds in 1957. -Kaston via Isham

52-9579 of Alabama's 160th TRS at Dannelly Field, Montgomery. During the squadron's T-33 era they flew a succession of RF-80As, RF-84Fs and RF-4Cs as their primary mission aircraft. -Olmsted

51-4157 as assigned to West Virginia's 167th FBS. It had previously been one of the initial batch transferred to Canada, as their number 14691. It eventually became a display aircraft at Cumberland, Maryland. -Smith

53-4903 with its original 168th FIS paint scheme. It has blue tip tank and rudder flashes, blue, red, blue nose bands. When the 168th was inactivated in 1958 it was transferred to the 108th FIS, also at O'Hare IAP. -Krieger via Olson

49-880 was originally delivered to the 3525th PTW at Williams AFB on March 3, 1949. After serving with two ATC Wings, two AFRES Wings, and two previous ANG squadrons, it finally was assigned in 1958 to the 169th FBS at Peoria, Illinois. In December 1961 it was sent to Davis-Monthon AFB, Arizona for storage, and later salvage. -Stevens

53-5323 of the 170th TFS at Capital Airport, Springfield, Illinois with one of its many paint scheme incarnations, this time totally devoid of any character besides having its lower fuselage painted gray. -Stevens

57-580 belonged to Michigan's 171st FIS at Selfridge ANGB. It was lost in a crash on September 14, 1981. -Barbier via Isham

A variation on the checkerboard paint scheme, this T-33A also belonged to Michigan's 171st FIS at Selfridge. -Strandberg via Isham

The 175th FIS, South Dakota ANG, was initially commanded by the legendary Marine Corps ace Joseph Foss. This T-Bird was named "Miss Monitor." -Paulson via Isham

Some T-33s certainly got around. This example originally was assigned to the Illinois ANG, serving in the two Chicago squadrons. It then went to Iowa's 124th FIS, and finished its career with Wisconsin's 176th FIS at Madison. Upon its withdrawal from service it became a display aircraft at Madison. -Taylor via Dorr

53-5944 of the 176th FIS at Madison was photographed at Truax ANGB on May 21, 1961. The rib construction of the flaps are shown to advantage. Modelers note that the tailpipe protrudes 6" beyond the aft fuselage. The badge shape panel below the canopy frame contains a mechanical canopy jettison lanyard for emergency entrance to the cockpit. -Stevens

Another 176th FIS T-Bird at Truax ANGB. Under the left wing is an ALQ-72 Electronic Counter Measures, ECM, pod; while under the right wing is a chaff dispenser. At this time the 176th was flying F-102As under the radio callsign of "Ram" (Raggidy-Assed Militia). -Winter

The "Happy Hooligans" are the 178th FIS, North Dakota ANG, who flew under the radio callsign of "NoDak." A rowdy bunch, they are best known for excelling as the best ANG interceptor squadron over the years. -Tenby via Isham

Montana's ANG aircraft always bore attractive paint schemes. "Big Sky Country" is a definite point of pride with them. The 120th FIG, 186th FIS was flying F-106As at the time of this photo. -Teuby via Isham

52-9654 of Wyoming's 187th FIS at Cheyenne. The 187th flew F-51Ds, and later F-80Cs and F-86Ls as a FIS before converting to MC-119Js in 1961 and becoming an air evacuation squadron. -Baker via Olson

The ANG takes great pride in the appearance of their aircraft, as this highly polished example belonging to the 194th FIS at Fresno, California shows. -Oruzolowski via Isham

53-5199 was transferred to the 194th FIS from Vermont's 134th FIS. It was photographed at Barksdale AFB, Louisiana in 1984. By this time the Air Defense Command had been inactivated and its committed squadrons assigned to the Tactical Air Command, hence TAC's insignia on its vertical stabilizer. -Sibert

52-9744 of the 196th FIS at Ontario, California. The 196th had been one of six ANG Fighter Bomber Squadrons to see combat in Korea during the Korean War, and then they returned to fly F-51Hs, F-86As and Ls, and F-102As during their T-33 era. -Kasulka via Esposito

52-9542 of Arizona's 197th "Copperheads" at Sky Harbor Airport, Phoenix. This squadron had an ADC role until 1962 when they converted to C-97Cs and became an ATS; then -9542 was sent to the 110th TFS at Lambert Field, St. Louis, Missouri. -Esposito

Another 196th FIS T-Bird at Ontario with a TF-102A "Tub" in the background. The red cap between the "F" and the "O" on its nose covers louvers utilized to help cool the nose bay avionics. -Hughes via Isham

The Far East Air Force (FEAF) and Pacific Air Force (PACAF)

Commencing in January 1950 T-33As were assigned to the Far East Air Force to enhance jet transition training in the three USAF fighter wings then flying F-80s in Japan, the 8th, and 49th Fighter Bomber Wings, and the 35th Fighter Interceptor Wing. Immediately following this action, further T-33s were assigned to the 51st Fighter Interceptor Wing on Okinawa and to the 18th Fighter Bomber Wing in the Philippine Islands. Then, with the outbreak of the Korean war, all five of these units found themselves involved in combat action, flying combat missions either from Japan or Korea, itself. As the war progressed three more combat units with T-33s were added to the combat roster, the 4th FIW, the 27th FEW and the 67th TRW. These were later supplemented by ancillary USAF fighter squadrons that rotated in and out of Korea, as the 68th and 319th Fighter-All Weather Squadrons, for example. Rotational duties also saw the T-33s of the 27th FEW assigned to replacement units, as the 136th FBW, who were in turn replaced by by the 58th FBW. During the course of the war T-33s were utilized in various roles, including weather and tactical reconnaissance, and at least two T-33s were lost on combat missions. On July 1, 1957 FEAF was disestablished and replaced by the Pacific Air Force, headquartered in Hawaii and now responsible for the largest geographical Theater in the USAF. Although T-33s were not actively involved in the Vietnam War, they did continue in their support function until after the war was brought to its conclusion, primarily in providing a vehicle for pilot proficiency.

A veteran of two wars, 49-966 initially saw action with the 35th FIW in Korea, and then was assigned to the 67th TRW on February 24, 1951. Over a decade later it was assigned to the 405th Fighter Wing at Clark Air Base, Philippines and it was salvaged in 1964. -Stoltz via Thompson

49-988 of the 8th Fighter Bomber Group at Taegu. In September 1950 it was transferred to the 49th FBG and it was lost on a weather reconnaissance mission on May 16, 1951, killing Lt. Colonel's Walter Selenger and Leland Molland. Selenger had been a charter member of the original F-80 Acrojets, and Molland was the temporary commanding officer of the 49th FBG. -O'Donnell

49-993 belonged to Headquarters 5th Air Force in Japan. Photographed at Taegu, it went missing on November 5, 1950 and was later found to have crashed, its loss being listed as an accident. -Brackenreg

49-971 was assigned to the 49th FBG on January 17, 1951 after being moved to Korea from the 18th Fighter Bomber Wing in the Philippine Islands. (The 18th FBG, itself, was heavily involved in Korean War combat at the time, only they were flying Mustangs). In 1954 it was returned to the 18th FBW and ended its career with the 405th FW at Clark Air Base. -Major via Thompson

"Black Sheep" was 49-983 of the 49th FBW's 8th FBS at Taegu in 1951. Note that it still does not have ejection seats installed and carries the "Misawa" tip tanks that were developed for the F-80 in Japan in January 1950. -Butcher

49-994 as assigned to the 8th FBW, 36th FBS, in their squadron colors. Based at Itazuke, Japan during this portion of the Korean War, it was lost in an accident near Itazuke on July 6, 1951 with both pilots being killed. -Miller via Isham

Assigned to the squadron commander of the 35th FBS, 8th FBW at K-13, (Suwon) in 1951 51-4484 has both ejection seats and the new Fletcher tip tanks. -Durkes via Thompson

"Black Sheep" was the moniker for 49-983 when it served with the 8th FBW in Korea. In 1953 it was transferred to the 49th FBW. -via Menard

51-8715 of the 58th FBW's 310th FBS in 1954. Based at Taegu, the Wing was in the process of converting from F-84Gs to F-86Fs. Unusual is that the "United States Air Force" is spelled out on the upper surface of the right wing. -Charles Trask via Menard

A world traveler. After an initial assignment to the Luftwaffe in Germany as their AB 785, 55-4421 was returned to the USAF and modified to AT-33 standards, and then it was assigned to PACAF's 405th Fighter Wing, who were involved with tactical training of foreign pilots, among other things. -Besecker via Paul

51-6620 of Headquarters Pacific Air Command at Hickam Air Force Base, Hawaii. while shooting touch-and-goes. Delivered to the USAF on July 8, 1952 it had served with the 27th FEW in Japan and the 51st FIW in Korea before its transfer to Hawaii. -Williams

55-4420 of Headquarters PACAF departing Hickam AFB on a practice radar interception mission with two chaff tanks and a radar reflector pod. The F-117 has nothing on the T-33 when it comes to trying to find one on radar with an inoperative transponder. -Williams

Equipped with a yellow ECM pod under its fuselage, this PACAF T-33A-15 departs Hickam AFB on a practice interception mission. It also has the new TACAN navigational antenna installed below the air intakes. -Williams

With the front pilot acting as a safety observer, this T-Bird is making a practice instrument takeoff from Hickam AFB with the backseat pilot under the IFR hood. -Williams

Assigned to Headquarters 5th Air Force, now under PACAF, 57-740 was photographed at Atsugi Air Base, Japan. It has the latest canopy breaker style ejection seats installed. -Williams

Assigned to an unknown PACAF unit at Yokota Air Base, Japan, 57-740 was photographed while landing on May 17, 1965 after an air defense exercise. -Matsuzaki via Isham

57-538 of PACAF in the last markings applied to their T-Birds. The canopy is covered with an aluminum blanket to retard sun and heat damage in the cockpit. -Williams

A PACAF T-33A venting pooled fuel via its sabre drain from its aft fuselage while on the pitch-out from the initial approach to landing at Hickam AFB. It looks scary but it is a non-emergency event. -Williams

The United States Air Force in Europe (USAFE)

The first assignment of the T-33 to USAF units in Europe was in June 1949 with the delivery of one example to the 36th Fighter Bomber Wing at Furstenfeldbruck Air Base, Germany by the 56th Fighter Group as a part of their Fox Able II Shooting Star mission, which was the first transatlantic delivery of jet fighters by air. This was followed on July 22, 1950 by eight more ex 56th Fighter Group T-Birds that were then assigned to various Air Bases in England and Germany.

Future T-33 deliveries to the USAFE would continue for the next decade, to meet the demand for jet training aircraft within various USAF units and for use in the other sundry roles that the T-Bird had found itself so versatile. For a short period even the previously disbanded Acrojets were reborn in September 1954 at Furstenfeldbruck by Major Michael Stolen, commanding officer of the 7330th Pilot Training Squadron. Stolen had been a member of the original Acrojets, and the PTS was charged with training foreign pilots under Mutual Defense Aid Pact requirements.

T-33A 49-1000 of the 513th Fighter Bomber Squadron at Manston with red tip tanks, the squadron's color. It crashed into the English Channel on November 20, 1952, but both crew members survived. -via Curtis

The next T-33A in construction sequence, 49-1001 belonged to the 81st Fighter Bomber Wing at Shepards Grove, England. Ejection seats have now been installed. The small U. S. Air Force on the fuselage is non standard. -Curtis

49-1006 of the 514th FBS, 406th FBW out of Manston on August 5, 1952 sans tip tanks. Note the crude application of the star in the National Insignia. Note the absence of ejection seats even at this late date, and the awkward posture of the pilots. It eventually went to Holland for use as spare parts. -Markowitz via Curtis

The remains of 51-4469 of the 514th, now a Fighter Interceptor Squadron, having switched from F-84Es to F-86Ds. It crashed at Wheelus Air Base, Lybia and the pilot escaped without injury, while the backseater suffered severe burns. -Torres via Curtis

51-8756 as assigned to the 20th Tactical Fighter Wing at Weathersfield, England with a non-standard application of the Buzz Numbers behind the fuselage National Insignia. It crashed on takeoff on Easter Sunday 1957. -Gradidge via Olson

51-8756 under salvage at the atomic research facility at Harwell, England after an unsuccessful attempt at a JATO takeoff. It was repaired and eventually transferred to Holland for service as a training aid. -via Curtis

52-9815 belonged to the 401st FBW, 613th FBS while on a TDY to Torrejon Air Base, Spain. The 401st FBW markings closely resembled those used by the 51st FIW in Korea. -Isham

52-9866 belonged to an unidentified USAF unit. It was photographed in Sweden after inadvertently landing there, due to a navigational error. It has unusually large Buzz Numbers. -Dorr

53-5133 of the 79th FBS, 20th FBW at Blackbushe, England with an apparently unremarkable scheme, but it actually bears an European font to the Buzz Numbers. It was transferred via MDAP to Spain on October 31, 1964 and became their E.15-57. -via Curtis

53-5144 of the 81st FBW at Woodbridge, England in 1957. Their insignia represents their nuclear capability. It later went to France, and eventually Singapore as number 908. -Pennick via Esposito

57-699 belonged to the 7101st Support Group at Wiesbaden Air Base, Germany in 1959. Its colors are unknown. -Menard

49-1002 had been one of the Fox Able II T-33s delivered to the 86th Fighter Bomber Wing. Shown here, it later belonged to the 50th FBW at Hahn Air Base, Germany. It was lost in a crash in November 1961. -Menard

Another 50th FBW T-33 at Hahn AB with revised markings. -Menard

The same 53-5050 with yet another set of identifying markings for the 50th FBW. The tail bands are in the colors of the Wing's three operational squadrons. Blue (10th FBS), yellow (81st FBS), and red (417th FBS). -Menard

50-370 of the 50th FBW. The Wing's motto under the fin insignia is "Master of the Sky." This T-33 now belongs to the Museum of Flying, Santa Monica, California as N651. -Menard

Flying the T-Bird

Starting with the customary walk-around, one makes sure that the landing gear shock struts are properly inflated, the air intakes are clear of foreign objects, and all of the control surfaces are free from binding, just like any other aircraft. But there are two critical items to be carefully checked. These are that the nose armament bay doors are securely latched, lest the doors open in flight. If they do, they create a drastically adverse airflow over the aircraft's wings and empennage, which can create a massive controllability problem. The other item is the fuselage fuel tank filler cap, located just aft of the canopy. If this cap is not properly seated, fuel will siphon from the tank and flow into the plenum chamber through the spring-loaded doors on the top of the center fuselage. If this occurs, the pilot is faced with only the narrow chance that a sufficient air speed will be attained to close these doors before a catastrophic explosion results.

Completing the walk-around the retaining safety pins are removed from the landing gear, which prevent an inadvertent ground gear retraction, and from the tip tanks, which prevent an inadvertent jettisoning of the same.

Likewise, upon entering the cockpit and completing the initial instrument and before takeoff checks and starting the engine, the ejection seat pins are removed, counted to make sure that all have been removed, and shown to the crew chief as a double check. It is most embarrassing to take off and not be able to retract the landing gear because a safety pin has not been withdrawn. The ejection seats are vertically adjustable for comfort, while the rudder pedals are also adjustable for length for reaching the toe brakes.

Starting the J33 engine is straight forward, and in warm weather it can be accomplished on the aircraft's internal battery. In colder temperatures, and as a matter of course, however, an Auxiliary Power Unit, APU, is used. The T-33 does have two male APU plugs installed for starting in extremely cold conditions, so that two APUs can be plugged in at the same time for below zero degree starts. With the electrical power turned on, the throttle is advanced to twenty percent to provide a "cool start." The cool start brings an equalized engine temperature to 540 degrees centigrade, and tailpipe temperature is not to exceed 696 degrees C. If 900 degrees C is reached, this is a "hot start," which requires an engine shut down and inspection for damage. Often when the engine is started with a wind blowing up the tailpipe, the unburned fuel in the exhaust gases can torch out the tailpipe, which, although spectacular, is not extraordinary.

It is said of all T-33 pilots that there are those who have and those who will, and this refers to the cocking of the nose wheel. The nose wheel is of the castoring type, whereupon ground direction is provided by differential braking. Too much of a turn and a stomp on a brake will cock the wheel to the offending side. It is possible to rock the aircraft via throttle application and a stomping of the brakes to release the weight on the nose wheel strut and straighten the aircraft, but the easiest—and most embarrassing way—is to call for assistance and have a strong back lift the weight off the nose strut to straighten the wheel. The ground is not a place to dilly-dally in a T-Bird, for it consumes 1.2 gallons a minute while just sitting there. Just prior to takeoff the engine is run up to 90% to check the oil pressure, and then she is ready to go.

With the flaps set at thirty-two degrees, commencing the takeoff begins with advancing the throttle to sixty percent with the emergency fuel pump on, along with gang loading the fuel tanks selector switch so that all the internal fuel tanks are on, permitting both the main and emergency electric fuel pumps to draw fuel from any or all tanks. (Except the tip tanks, which are driven by compressed engine air pressure. The tip tank system is designed, accordingly, to maintain a balance between the tip tanks, so if one fails to feed, the other will not, which would otherwise create an asymmetrical balance problem. Faced with this situation, a pilot can either elect to effect a "heavy landing," or jettison the tip tanks). With the fuel system operating properly, power is increased to one hundred percent. At sea level under normal conditions a takeoff run of 3,540 feet is to be anticipated to clear the standard 50 foot obstacle, but depending on the airfield's altitude and/or density altitude, this distance can be increased by 25 percent. Acceleration is smooth, but not spectacular, with direction accomplished through differential braking. The seldom used rudder becomes effective at fifty knots, and the elevators at seventy knots. The nose wheel is raised at ninety knots, and liftoff under standard weights and conditions is at one hundred ten knots, at which time the landing gear is retracted, along with retracting the flaps to fifteen degrees until one hundred-forty knots is attained. Absolutely no maneuver is attempted until this magic speed is reached. 140 knots is considered the minimum safe airspeed at all altitudes. With a takeoff weight of 15,000 pounds, including 810 gallons of JP-4 fuel (4,860 pounds), the engine "spool-up" time of fifteen seconds has to be kept in mind at all times. One can never let themselves get behind the proverbial power curve in the T-33.

With the aileron boost pumps on, and the absence of a conventional airplane's torque, the T-Bird's flight characteristics are smooth through all normal maneuvers. But the T-33 does have a tendency to have a wing wobble until the pilot gets used to the light aerodynamic forces on the ailerons. These boost pumps are one of the better jokes in T-Bird lore, for with a diminutive pilot in the front seat and an uninitiated observer in the back, some fun can be had. The pilot can smoothly roll and turn the T-33 with ease with the pumps on, and then the passenger is invited to try his hand at flying the aircraft while the pilot surreptitiously turns the pumps off. The stick may well be set in concrete, for even the strongest individual has a difficult time in overcoming the aerodynamic forces on the ailerons.

Although flight visibility is limited from the cockpit, as the pilot's shoulders are barely above the canopy sill and there is little space to move one's head about, flying the aircraft through the standard regimes is enjoyable and without difficulty. All of the basic acrobatic maneuvers are permitted, with inverted flight being limited to thirty seconds because of the oil system.

At altitude the T-33 is faced with the problem of "Coffin Corner," much like the straight wing F-84 was, but to a lesser degree than the Thunderjet pilots had to contend with. The relationship between the T-33's critical Mach of .80 and compressibility above 30,000 feet is quite close. As the aircraft is aerodynamically clean, it is easy to get to the point of getting it to go too fast at altitude, which then, through compressibility, creates an airframe buffeting and renders the elevator control surfaces ineffective. Too much speed and the aircraft's nose will start to tuck under, which increases the speed, bringing on more of a tuck under tendency. As the speed builds up, more and more altitude and Gs must be pulled for recovery. Four Gs at 505 knots from 30,000 feet will require 10,000 in altitude to recover from a dive, while at 6 Gs, some 6,500 feet are required. However, by pulling these high Gs airframe structural limitations can easily be exceeded at either speed or altitude, as each increase in G forces reduces the allowable attainable airspeed by five knots. Even though the T-33 is built to the standard military requirement of being able to withstand 7.33 positive Gs and 3 negative ones (Lockheed actually built it to 11 positive and 5 negative!), if one is not careful one can easily overstress the aircraft by creating something between skin wrinkles and total destruction.

Landing the T-33 is again basically straight forward. The initial approach speed was at the pilot's whim before the FAA imposed the 250 knots below 10,000 feet rule, and the "break" from initial to downwind also depended on the pilot's mood and his desire to pull the standard 3 Gs and look sharp on the pitch-out, or just take it easy around the pattern. The desired downwind speed is 185 knots, so the speed boards are popped at this time. Just prior to turning the base leg the landing gear is lowered and given a "jiggle check," as the handle is much like an old fashioned gearshift and is long and springy, and there is no definite physical indication that it has done its intended job. The flaps are then dropped to 50% (thirty degrees), and then the base is turned with a desired speed of 150 knots. The pilot shoots for 125 knots on final, and 110 knots "over the fence." This last turn from base to final is critical for lining up with the runway. The early T-33s with the underslung tip tanks could safely be cross-controlled to side-slip into alignment with the runway, but the modification to the centerline type tanks created a situation where in a side-slip of more than thirty degrees the airflow over the side of the tip tanks blanked out aileron effectiveness at this most critical point, and several pilots were killed before the problem was recognized. Touchdown is at 90 knots, which gives a ten knot margin over the normal landing weight stall speed of 80 knots. By clearing the proverbial 50 foot obstacle on final, a landing run of 3,100 feet is to be anticipated.

In the final flare for landing the T-33 can enter a critical situation as it enters into ground effect and has a tendency to float if the airspeed has not been managed properly. The F-80/T-33/F-94 series brought an entirely new term into the lexicon with the advent of the "JC" maneuver. Here the aircraft has a tendency to porpoise, with ever increasing amplitude as the pilot attempts to chase the climbing or plunging T-Bird, and he will always be on the wrong side of the arc. The only answer is "Jesus Christ!," center and hold the stick, and allow the aircraft to fly itself out of harms way.

Other Duties

The T-33 was nothing if not a versatile aircraft that was used by the USAF and other military services and agencys in just about every form imaginable. It served as a "hack" for transportation of personnel and small parts on a continuing basis throughout its service life. Likewise, with its easily adapted nose section and cockpit, it was readily adapted for many further roles.

48-919 was assigned to the 2760th Air Base Unit at Clinton County AFB, Ohio under Project AMC-9PF-78 on February 18, 1949. This unit supported the Air Force's All-Weather Flying Center for thunderstorm research. It sported a red nose with yellow piping, likewise, the tip tanks are red and the vertical fin and wing tips are red with a yellow chevron, the general markings of the AWFC. -Isham

The same 48-919 in a later incarnation as a JT-33A, having spent its entire career in various research roles and modes, previously having been designated as an EQT-33A. Here it bears the nose of a TM-76 Mace. -Olsen

48-360 was delivered to the USAF on September 27, 1948 and on March 31, 1949 it became the first DTF-80C assigned to the 2754th Air Base Group at Holloman AFB, New Mexico. The "D" prefix denoted Drone Director. -Baker via Paul

50-383 was delivered to the USAF on December 11, 1950 and initially assigned to Wright Patterson AFB, Ohio, On June 4, 1952 it was then assigned to the 3205th Drone Group at Holloman AFB and became a DT-33. In October 1954 it was transferred to the 3200th Proof Test Group at Eglin AFB. -Holmquist via Olson

49-920, an EDT-33A after modification to a drone controller by the Sperry Corporation, Geneva, New York. It was assigned to the 3200th Target and Drone Squadron, Eglin AFB, Florida under project Bad Boy, which also concerned the QF-80. It also served in the atomic test programs at Eniwetok Atoll. Note the extra antennas on its nose and aft fuselage. - Gordon Williams via Olson

FAA T-Bird, ex BuAer 128671 (51-4293). They were used for high altitude flight checking of navigational aids and as general hacks. -Lockheed

A drone director DT-33 with a QF-80 under guidance, although the Shooting Star's cockpit is occupied by a pilot. -via Menard

A U. S. Navy TV-2KD, the radio controlled target modification of the TV-2. The Navy had at least thirty-two of these, of which the survivors were redesignated as DT-33Bs in 1962. Note all the dorsal and ventral antennas, along with an arrestor hook, lest the aircraft become wayward on the runway. -U. S. Navy

Civilian registered as N1449, s/n unknown, this T-Bird belonged to the U. S. Geological Survey, Water Resources Division. -MAP via Hansen

An ex U. S. Navy T-33A in the possession of the Federal Aviation Agency. The FAA's T-Birds had been stored at NAS Litchfield Park, near Davis Monthon AFB, Arizona for a period before being taken over by the FAA in the late 1950s. -MAP via Hansen

Civilian T-Birds

The Lockheed T-33 became popular as a civilian testbed aircraft with several firms that had obtained government contracts for development programs; as Bob Laidlaw's Flight Systems Incorporated and Flight Test Incorporated and their subsidiary, Russ O'Quinn's Aeronautical Specialties Inc. in the early 1970s. These firms seemed to have an inside track on obtaining these aircraft from surplus USAF and Canadian stocks, and purchased several "blocks" of them, and had them numbered in a numerical sequence. Warbird dealer Leroy Penhall imported thirteen examples, and kept N12413 for himself. Later on in the 1970s these same aircraft were sold on the pure civilian market, as they were becoming popular on the "warbird" scene. They were relatively inexpensive, particularly in comparison to some as the P-51 Mustang, whose prices were increasing by leaps, and T-33 parts were still plentiful and inexpensive. As time and ownership have passed, many of these T-Birds have been sold and resold, registered and reregistered, to a point where one needs the proverbial scorecard to keep track of them. Particularly those whose owners have confused their serial numbers through a mix of USAF or Canadian serials over the years. Nevertheless, the T-33 has proven itself to be a viable, and especially, safe aircraft for civilian operation. Its presence at an airshow is particularly welcome for its appearance and historical importance.

N32GB is 53-6091, one of the few civilian registered ex USAF aircraft. Previously it had been an instructional airframe at Lewis College, Lockport, Illinois where it was registered as N91189. -Phillips

N33VC is one of the few civilian T-Birds in European skies. It was one of the first civilian T-33s, initially having been CF-IAB, then, G-OHAB and G-Jett. It is now registered as G-TBRD. -Phillips

Another view of N33VC, ex RCAF 21261, and based at Duxford, England. It was previously owned by Ormond Haydon-Baillie, and now belongs to the Old Flying Machine Company. -Curtis

N72JR being refueled. As a laborious task for civilians as it was for the military, with five major fuel tanks requiring attention. Certainly a beautiful paint job. Its positive identification is unknown, for its serial number is only listed as "295." -Phillips

N83TB, ex RCAF 21559. Previously it was registered as N3370. -Haag via Williams

N109X as belonging to Flight Test Research, Long Beach, California in 1977. It is ex RCAF 21298, and now is registered in Canada as CF-SCJ. -Williams

Another view of N109X with a modified paint scheme when it belonged to Flight Test Research. -Centurion via Davis

With a similar paint scheme, N156X was RCAF 21192, and it was later reregistered as N304FS. -Williams

N157X with a variation of Flight Test Research's paint scheme. It was later registered as N302FS. It is ex RCAF 21024. -Williams

Continuing in the series, N158X is RCAF 21546. It was later registered as NX333JM. Note that the IFR hood is closed to keep the cockpit a little cooler. -Williams

N123MJ, ex USAF 51-9127, belongs to the American Air Museum, Oakland, California. -Haag via Williams

N123MJ with a more modern appearing paint scheme. A shame that the back seat is vacant! -Phillips

The Blue Angels TV-2 made a good paint scheme for a civilian warbird. N304FS was previously N156X. -Phillips

N306FS of Flight Systems Incorporated at Mojave, California. It is ex RCAF 21306, ex N99193. Here modified for some esoteric research program. Note the "eightball" on the nose. -Davis

Bearing the markings of the Strategic Air Command, N306FS is actually ex RCAF 21306 that had previously been registered as N99173. -Phillips

Another Blue Angels look-alike. NX333MJ. The Angels flew three different TV-2s, and the scheme is legitimate. -Phillips

N12413, ex N21273. It was written off in an accident on May 4, 1990. -Wooley via Isham

Painted as a Red Knight of the Canadian acrobatic team, N12413 was ex RCAF 21273. -Kennedy via Phillips

N12414, ex RCAF 21160. Photographed at Addison, Texas August 15, 1981. -Haag via Williams

N12418, ex RCAF 21265, landing at Breckenridge, Texas on May 28, 1994. -Phillips

N12418 at Breckenridge. It crashed at Selfridge ANGB, Michigan during an airshow on June 11, 1994. Pilot / owner Ray Mabrey perished: A heart attack was suspected. -Phillips

Ex Royal Canadian Navy 21341, now registered as N12422. After being assigned to HMCS Shearwater's VU 32 it became one of the Golden Hawk's hacks before being sold as surplus. -Phillips

N64666, ex RCAF 21129. It has since been registered as N84TB. -Haag via Williams

N99175, ex RCAF 21557. Previously it had been one of Canada's versions of the RT-33. Here it is resplendent in the markings of the Golden Hawks. -Kennedy via Phillips

Another Red Knight look alike, one of the more famous and spectacular T-33 paint schemes. NX99184, ex RCAF 21098. -Kennedy via Phillips

N99185, ex RCAF 21236, painted in the markings of 414 Squadron, the "Black Knights." -via Phillips

G-OAHB, ex RCAF 21261 and CF-IHB in the markings utilized by O. A. Haydon-Baillie, one of the first foreign owners of civilian T-33s. (He died in a P-51 crash). This is of two T-33s with a German registry. -Pennick via Davis.

The T-33 soldiers on. N12416, ex RCAF 21369, now belongs to Boeing. Here, in 1998, it is being evaluated to provide a baseline in radar cross-section signature as a new radar system is being developed for the F-22 Raptor. -Mike Tull

G-TJet, ex USAF 51-8566 in the attractive markings of an instrument trainer belonging to the 36th Fighter Bomber Group when they flew the T-Bird from Furstenfeldbruck AB, Germany in 1952. -Phillips

Preserved and Display T-Birds

With the possible exception of the F-84 series, there are probably more T-33s on display as memorials, gate guards and museum aircraft than any other type of aircraft. Including several examples that were also supplied to trade schools for use as instructional airframes, and later placed on display, there were no less than 267 examples donated by the U. S. Military and the Canadian armed forces for display. As time has passed this number has diminished, for acts of vandalism or apathy in maintaining the aircraft has since seen may of these rendered junk and relegated to scrap yards. Many of the existing T-33s are mere hulks, lacking engines and ejection seats, and you can see right through them from one end to another! Nevertheless, a maintained T-33 is a viable museum piece and worth of a visit.

At NAS Willow Grove, Pennsylvania BuAer 138048. It appears that some damage has occurred to the aft portion of the canopy and a patch has been placed over the hole. -U.S. Navy via Dorr

At the Tallmantz Museum, John Wayne Airport, Orange County, California in 1965. 55-5341 had served with the Air Research and Development Command. -Williams

52-9734 was the last operational Air Defense Command T-33, having been retired from the 48th Fighter Interceptor Squadron at Langley AFB, Virginia. It is on display at Hampton, Virginia. -Dorr

52-9502 on display at the American Legion Post, Paris, Illinois. Placing them on a pylon helps keep them out of harms way. -Fisher

T-33A 51-9036 was a ex French Air Force T-Bird. It was undergoing restoration at the Newark Air Museum, England in 1980. -Curtis

51-17431, a T-33A-1LO. Previously of the Military Air Transport Command, it is on display at Dover AFB, Delaware. It bears the old MATS insignia on its fuselage, and the later Military Airlift Command insignia on its vertical fin. -Corbell via Williams

52-9326, "Big Mac" on display at Covington, Indiana. -Fisher

53-5933 outside of the Confederate Air Force hanger at Smartt Field, St. Charles, Missouri. It had previously served with the 175th FIS, but bears the markings of the 110th TFS. Previously it had been displayed at Jonesboro, Arkansas. -McLaren

With an erroneous serial number of 55-9797, this T-Bird is actually 52-9797. It is on display at the old Chanute AFB, Illinois. -McLaren

At Winona, Minnesota is 57-9622, registered as N86905 and belonging to the Winona Vocational Technical School. -Phillips

56-1573, an ex PACAF T-Bird at a technical school in Honolulu, Hawaii. —Williams

How not to treat a lady! 53-5853 at Ford Island, Hawaii. It had been used as a prop for the film Tora Tora Tora. -Williams

T-33/TV-2 Aircraft

For the USAF these aircraft were initially produced in "Block" series as either T-33A-1s or T-33A-5s, depending on whether they were capable of having the .50 caliber nose armament installed, or not. These Block numbers were later expanded to denote modifications to the navigational equipment, etc. The U. S. Navy TO-2/TV-2 series utilized a different system to denote internal aircraft revisions, using a lower case letter instead. These letters are reflected on the end of the appropriate BuAer numbers.

Air Force serial number	Lockheed Construction number	Navy BuAer Number	Quantity Built
Contract AC 19283 (172 examples)			
T-33A-1 ff.			
48-356/375	5001/5020		
(48-356/373 to YF-94)			20
48-913/920	5021/5028		8
49-879/933	5029/5083		55
49-934	5084	124570a	1
49-935/1006	5085/5156		72
49-2757	5157		1
49-2758/2772	5158/5172	124571/124585b	15
Contract AC 9205 (139 examples, including those listed below)			
50-320/327	5173/5180		8
50-328/329	5181/5182	124930/124931c	2
50-330/337	5183/5190		8
50-338/342	5191/5195	124932/124936d	5
50-343/348	5196/5201		6
50-349/351	5202/5204	124937/124939e	3
50-352/431	5205/5284		80
Contract AF 14806			
50-432	5528		1
Contract AF 9205			
50-433/454	5286/5307		22
50-1272/1276	5308/5312		5
Contract AF 14806 (977 examples, including 50-432)			
51-4019/4024	5313/5318	126583/126588f	6
51-4025/4030	5319/5324		6
51-4031/4036	5325/5330	126589/126594f	6
51-4037/4051	5331/5345		15
51-4052/4057	5346/5351	1265951126600g	6
51-4058/4077	5352/5371		20
51-4078/4083	5372/5377	126601/126606g	6
51-4084/4103	5378/5397		20
51-4104/4109	5398/5403	126607/126612h	6
51-4110/4136	5404/5430		27
51-4137/4142	5431/5436	126613/126618h	6
51-4143/4173	5437/5467		31

51-4174/4179	5468/5473	126619/126624i	6
51-4180/4233	5474/5527		54
51-4234/4236	5529/5531		3
51-4237/4238	5532/5533	126625/126626i	2
51-4239/4243	5534/5538	128661/128665i	5
51-4244/4287	5539/5582		44
51-4288/4294	5583/5589	128666/128672j	7
51-4295/4354	5590/5649		60
51-4355/4364	5650/5659	128673/128682k	10
51-4365/4424	5660/5719		60
51-4425/4434	5720/5729	128683/128692l	10
51-4435/4514	5730/5809		80
51-4515/4524	5810/5819	128693/128702l	10
51-4525/4533	5820/5828		9
51-6497/6577	5829/5909		81
51-6578/6587	5910/5919	128703/128712l	10
51-6588/6664	5920/5996		77
51-6665/6674	5997/6006	128713/128722m	10
51-6675/6957	6007/6289		283

Contract AF 23071 (825 examples)

51-8506/8517	6290/6301		12
51-8518/8541	6302/6325	131725/131748n	24
51-8542/8635	6326/6419		94
51-8636/8651	6420/6435	131749/131764o	16
51-8652/8728	6436/6512		77
51-8729/8749	6513/6533	131765/131785o	21
51-8750/8835	6534/6619		86
51-8836/8870	6620/6654	131786/131820p	35
51-8871/8939	6655/6723		69
51-8940/8953	6724/6737	131821/131834p	14
51-8954/9039	6738/6823		86
51-9040/9075	6824/6859	131835/131870q	36
51-9076/9149	6860/6933		74
51-9150/9167	6934/6951	131871/131888q	18
51-9168/9310	6952/7094		143
51-16976/16995	7095/7114		20

Contract AF 6578 (1,110 examples)

51-17388/17409	7115/7136		22
51-17410/17443	7149/7182		34
51-17444/17455	7137/7148		12
51-17456/17467	7247/7258		12
51-17468/17486	7362/7380		19
51-17487/17511	7467/7491		25
51-17512117536	757217596		25
51-17537/17556	7682/7701		20
52-9129/9192	7183/7246		64
52-9193/9295	7259/7361		103
52-9296/9381	7381/7466		86
52-9382/9461	7492/7571		80
52-9462/9546	7597/7681		85
52-9547/9616	7707/7776		70
52-9617/9691	7802/7876		75
52-9692/9751	7917/7976		60
52-9752/9826	8012/8086		75
52-9827/9875	8133/8181		49
52-9876/9880	7702/7706		5

52-9881/9905	7777/7801		25
52-9906/9925	7877/7896		20
52-9926/9940	7977/7991		15
52-9941/9950	8087/8096		10
52-9951/9975	8182/8206		25
53-2687/2708	7897/7916	136793/136812r	20
53-2707/2726	7992/8011	136813/136832r	20
53-2727/2762	8097/8132	136833/136868s	36
53-2763/2780	8207/8224	136869/136886s	18

Contract AF 22282 (1, 267 examples)

53-4886/5240	8225/8579		355
(53-5090, 5174, 5209, 5237/5239 as RT-33A)			
53-5241/5243	8580/8582	137934/137936t	3
53-5244/5309	8583/8648		66
(53-5257, 5273, 5291, 5308 as RT-33A)			
53-5310/5317	8649/8656	137937/137944u	8
53-5318/5350	8657/8689		33
(53-5322, 5335, 5347 as RT-33A)			
53-5351/5358	8690/8697	137945/137952u	8
53-5359	8698		1
(RT-33A)			
53-5360/5363	8699/8702	137953/137956u	4
53-5364/5374	8703/8713		11
(53-5371 as RT-33A)			
53-5375/5383	8714/8722	137957/137965u	9
53-5384	8723		1
(RT-33A)			
53-5385/5387	8724/8726	137966/137968u	3
53-5388/5436	8727/8775		49
(53-5396, 5409, 5420, 5430 as RT-33A)			
53-5437/5440	8776/8779	137969/137972u	4
53-5441	8780		1
(RT-33A)			
53-5442/5448	87818787	137973/137979u	7
53-5449	8788		1
(RT-33A)			
53-5450/5456	8789/8795	137980/137986u	7
53-5457	8796		1
(RT-33A)			
53-5458/5460	8797/8799	137987/137989u	3
53-5461/5504	8800/8843		44
(53-5466, 5474, 5482, 5491, 5499 as RT-33A)			
53-5505/5507	8844/8846	137990/137992v	3
53-5508	8847		1
(RT-33A)			
53-5509/5516	8848/8855	137993/138000v	8
53-5517	8856		1
(RT-33A)			
53-5518/5524	8857/8863	138001/138007v	7
53-5525	8864		1
(RT-33A)			
53-5526/5532	8865/8871	138008/138014v	7
53-5533	8872		1
(RT-33A)			
53-5534	8873	138015v	1
53-5535/5569	8874/8908		35
(53-5539, 5546, 5553, 5560, 5567 as RT-33A)			
53-5570/5573	89098912	138016/138019v	4

53-5574	8913		1
(RT-33A)			
53-5575/5580	8914/8919	138020/138025v	6
53-5581	8920		1
(RT-33A)			
53-5582/5586	8921/8925	138026/138030v	5
53-5587	8926		1
(RT-33A)			
53-5588/5593	8927/8932	138031/138036v	6
53-5594	8933		1
(RT-33A)			
53-5595/5599	8934/8938	138037/138041v	5
53-5600	8939		1
(RT-33A)			
53-5601/5603	8940/8942	138042/138044v	3
53-5604/5641	8943/8980		38
(53-5607, 5613, 5619, 5626, 5631, 5638 as RT-33A)			
53-5642/5643	8981/8982	138045/138046v	2
53-5644	8983		1
(RT-33A)			
53-5645/5649	8984/8988	138047/138051v	5
53-5650	8989		1
(RT-33A)			
53-5651/5655	8990/8994	138052/138056v	5
53-5656	8995		1
(RT-33A)			
53-5657/5661	8996/9000	138057/138061v	5
53-5662	9001		1
(RT-33A)			
53-5663/5667	9002/9006	138062/138066w	5
53-5668	9007		1
(RT-33A)			
53-5669/5674	9008/9013	138067/138072w	6
53-5675	9014		1
(RT-33A)			
53-5676/5680	9015/9019	138073/138077w	5
53-5681	9020		1
(RT-33A)			
53-5682/5686	9021/9025	138078/138082w	5
53-5687	9026		1
(RT-33A)			
53-5688/5692	9027/9031	138083/138087w	5
53-5693	9032		1
(RT-33A)			
53-5694/5698	9033/9037	138088/138092w	5
53-5699	9038		1
(RT-33A)			
53-5700/5704	9039/9043	138093/138097w	5
53-5705	9044		1
(RT-33A)			
53-5706/5709	9045/9048	141490/141493w	4
53-5710	9049		1
(RT-33A)			
53-5711/5715	9050/9054	141494/141498w	5
53-5716	9055		1
(RT-33A)			
53-5717/5719	9056/9058	141499/141501w	3
53-5720/5799	9059/9138		80
(53-5721, 5727, 5733, 5739, 5745, 5751, 5756, 5763, 5768, 5773, 5779, 5785, 5790, 5795 as RT-33A)			
53-5800/5801	9157/9158		2

53-5802/5805	9160/9163		4
53-5806/5800	9165/9168		4
53-5810/5813	9170/9173		4
53-5814/5849	9215/9250		36
53-5850/5878	9291/9319		29
53-5879/5918	9355/9449		39

T-33A-5 ff.

53-5919/5973	9395/9449		54
53-9574/5993	9456/9475		19
53-5994/6037	9526/9569		44
53-6038/6066	9641/9669		29
53-6067/6152	9688/9773		86

Contract AF 26630 (145 examples)

T-33A-1 ff.

54-1522/1539	9139/9156		18
(54-1522, 1527, 1532, 1537 as RT-33A)			
54-1540	9159		1
(RT-33A)			
54-1541	9164		1
RT-33A)			
54-1542	9169		1
(RT-33A)			
54-1543	9174		1
(RT-33A)			
54-1544/1561	9175/9192		18
(54-1548, 1553 as RT-33A)			
54-1562/1583	9251/9272		22
54-1584/1618	9320/9354		35
54-2689/2710	9193/9214	138977/138998x	22
54-2711/2728	9273/9290	138999/139016x	18
54-2950/2955	9450/9455		6
54-4035/4036	9686/9687		2

Contract AF 30670 (18 examples)

55-2979/2983	9478/9480		5

(Except -2980, 2982. Including -3029, -3032, -3035, -3039, 3042, -3045, 3074, -3079, -3084, -3089, -3094, -3099, 3100, 3105, and -3110 from Contract AF 28429. All for Mutual Defense Aid Pact)

Contract AF 28429 (268 examples)

55-2984/3016	9481/9513	141502/141534y	33
(Includes -2980, 2982)			

T-33A-5 ff.

55-3017/3028	9514/9525		12

T-33A-1 ff.

55-3029/3049	9570/9590		21
55-3050/3073	9591/9614	141535/141558z	24
55-3074/3099	9615/9640		26
55-3100/3115	9670/9685		16

T-33A-5 ff.

55-3116/3117	9774/9775		2
55-4332/4424	9776/9868		103

T-33A-1 ff.

55-4425/4456	9869/9900		31
55-4807/4810	9901/9904		4
55-4945/4962	9905/9922		18

Contract AF 31212 (256 examples)

56-1573/1646	9923/9996		74
56-1647	9997	143014aa	1
56-1648/1649	9998/9999		2
56-1650	1000		1
56-1651	1001	143015aa	1
56-1652/1654	1002/1004		3
56-1655	1005	143016aa	1
56-1656/1658	1006/1008		3
56-1659	1009	143017aa	1
56-1660/1662	1010/1012		3
56-1663	1013	143018aa	1
56-1664/1666	1041/1016		3
56-1667	1017	143019aa	1
56-1668/1670	1018/1020		3
56-1671	1021	143020aa	1
56-1672/1674	1022/1024		3
56-1675	1025	143021aa	1
56-1676/1678	1026/1028		3
56-1679	1029	143022aa	1
56-1680/1682	10301032		3
56-1683	1033	143023aa	1
56-1684/1686	1034/1036		3
56-1687	1037	143024ab	1
56-16881690	10381040		3
56-1691	1041	143025ab	1
56-1692/1694	1042/1044		3
56-1695	1045	143026ab	1
56-1696/1698	1046/1048		3
56-1699	1049	143027ab	1
56-1700/1702	1050/1052		3
56-1703	1053	143028ab	1
56-1704/1706	1054/1056		3
56-1707	1057	143029ab	1
56-1708/1710	1058/1060		3
56-1711	1061	143030ab	1
56-1712/1714	1062/1064		3
56-1715	1065	143031ab	1
56-1716/1718	1066/1068		3
56-1719	1069	143032ab	1
56-1720/1722	1070/1072		3
56-1723	1073	143033ab	1
56-1724/1726	1074/1076		3
56-1727	1077	143034ab	1
56-1728/1730	1078/1080		3
56-1731	1081	143035ab	1
56-1732/1734	1082/1084		3
56-1735	1085	143036ab	1
56-1736/1738	1086/1088		3
56-1739	1089	143037ab	1
56-1740/1743	1090/1093		4
56-1744	1094	143038ab	1
56-1745/1747	1095/1097		3
56-1748	1098	143039ab	1

56-1749/1751	1099/1101		3
56-1752	1102	143040ab	1
56-1753/1755	1103/1105		3
56-1756	1106	143041ab	1
56-1757/1759	1107/1109		3
56-1760	1110	143042ab	1
56-1761/1763	1111/1113		3
56-1764	1114	143043ab	1
56-1765/1767	1115/1117		3
56-1768	1118	143044ab	1
56-1769/1771	1119/1121		3
56-1772	1122	143045ab	1
56-1773/1775	1123/1125		3
56-1776	1126	143046ab	1
56-1777/1779	1127/1129		3
56-1780	1130	143047ab	1
58-1781/1783	1131/1133		3
56-1784	1134	143048ab	1
56-1785/1787	1135/1137		3
56-1788	1138	143049ab	1
56-1789/1792	1139/1142		4

T-33A-5 ff

56-3659/3694	1143/1178		36
56-6848/6927	1179/1258		79

Contract AF 33550 (240 examples)

57-530/769	1179/1418		240

Contract AF 34659 (274 examples)

58-450/710	1419/1679		261
58-2094/2106	1680/1692		13

Total T-33/TV-2 Production 5, 691 examples

Note: TF-80C, cn 5018, 48-373, converted to YF-94A.

Canada

Canada received twenty T-33As, 50-429/430, -433, 51-1275/-1276, 51-4063/-4065, 51-4091/-4093, 51-4119, 51-4121, 51-4146, 51-4156, 51-6713/-6714, 51-6717, which they named as the "Silver Star," Mk. 1, and were given Royal Canadian Air Force Serial Numbers 14675/14694. Their 14695 was re-engined and identified as a Mk. 2, and it became the prototype Mk. 3.

Canadair then built 656 Mk. 3s, serialing 21001/21656, which were later redesignated as the CT-133 and re-serial numbered 133001/133656. Several of these Silver Stars were transfered to the Royal Canadian Navy, while surplus RCAF examples were supplied to various foreign air forces, notably France, Greece and Portugal. Over forty of the Canadair CT-133s have been sold as surplus on the civilian "Warbird" circuit.

Japan

Two T-33A were prepared for shipment to Japan by Lockheed Air Service: 54-1584 (cn 9320) and 54-1585 (cn 9321) to serve as pattern aircraft for their future construction by Kawasaki. Eighteen further examples were also shipped in kit form before their own construction got underway: 55-2979 (cn 9476), 55-2981 (cn 9478), 55-2983 (cn9480), 55-3029 (cn 9570), 55-3032 (cn 9573), 55-3035 (cn 9576), 55-3039 (cn 958O), 55-3042 (cn 9583), 55-3045 (cn 9586), 55-3074 (cn 9615), 55-3079 (cn 9620), 55-3084 (cn 9625), 55-3089 (cn 9630), 55-3094 (cn 9635), 55-3099 (cn 9640), 55-3100 (cn 9670), 55-3105 (cn 9675), 55-3110 (cn 9680).

Japanese serials for these aircraft are not known at this time.

Further Japanese construction produced 210 examples by Kawasaki between 1956 and 1959. 1956 production was serialed with 61-xxx, 1957 with 71-xxx, 1958 with 81-xxx, and 1959 with 91-xxx.

T2V-1 (Later T-1A)

1000	Prototype: identified as N125D	
1001/1008	142261/142268	8
1009/1011	142397/142399	3
1012/1020	142533/142541	9
1021/1120	144117/144216	100
1121/1150	144735/144764	30
	Total T2V-1 Production	150

Bibliography

Arnold, Rhoads, Shooting Star, T-Bird & Starfire, Tucson: Aztex Corporation, 1981

Chilstrom, Ken & Leary, Penn, ed. Test Flying at Old Wright Field. Omaha: Westchester House, 1993

Davis, Larry, P-80 Shooting Star in Action, Carrollton: Squadron/Signal Publications, 1980

Ferrer, Edward B. Operation Puma,International Aviation Consultants, Inc., Miami, 1982

Francillon, Rene J., The United States Air National Guard. London: Aerospace Publishing, 1993

Goldberg, Alfred, ed. A History of the United States Air Force 1907-1957, Trenton: D. Van Nostrad, 1957

Hallion, Richard P. "P-80: Story of a Star." Air Enthusiast, November 1979-February 1980, #11. Pg. 54

Lyzun, Jim "Pure Canadian Silver: Canada's T-Birds," Air Enthusiast, November-December 1997, #72, Pg. 68ff

Ravenstein, Charles A. Air Force Combat Wings 1947-1977. Washington: Office of Air Force History, 1984

Wooldridge, E. T. Jr., The P-80 Shooting Star: Evolution of a Jet Fighter, Washington: Smithsonion Institution Press, 1979

Also from the publisher

Lockheed
P-80/F-80
SHOOTING
STAR
FT-822
A PHOTO CHRONICLE
David R. McLaren
A SCHIFFER
MILITARY HISTORY
BOOK